HOLIDAYS BY COACH : An ill

ated history of Wallace Arnold

Stewart J. Brown

Contents

The line drawing above, and those which appear at intervals throughout this book, have been taken from Wallace Arnold brochures of the 1940s, 1950s and 1960s.

Robert Barr

ROBERT BARR, the founder of the Barr & Wallace Arnold Trust, was born in Edinburgh in 1889, the first son of a Scottish farming family. He was brought up at Woolley, near Wakefield. In 1904 he went to Leeds, becoming an apprentice at the Bridge Garage for 5s (25p) a week. Motor vehicles were still in their infancy. An apprenticeship with a motor engineer was a brave move. Who could be sure that these new-fangled, noisy, temperamental carriages would ever be popular?

In 1912 Barr bought his first vehicle, a Karrier which was used as a truck during the week and an open charabanc at weekends. He never looked back. Both his haulage and passenger fleets grew. The outbreak of World War II saw a change in the company's direction as pleasure traffic was halted and the company's coaches were diverted to essential work. Robert Barr, as one of the leading transport operators in Yorkshire, was appointed to act as regional transport co-ordinator for the Ministry of Transport - a role which he fitted alongside the control of his own businesses.

The nationalisation of the haulage industry after the war effectively brought to and end Robert Barr's haulage interests. After overseeing the postwar expansion of the company's coach operations, he turned his attention to expansion in other fields. Wallace Arnold Sales & Service was formed in the mid-1950s and developed into a major chain of profitable motor car dealerships. Robert Barr was chairman of the Barr & Wallace Arnold Trust from 1937 until his death in July 1961.

Front cover: The Volvo B10M with Plaxton's stylish Excalibur body is typical ofthe high-quality coaches being operated by Wallace Arnold in the 1990s. The Duple-bodied Leyland Tiger shown in the inset was equally the last word in luxury in the late1930s.
Main picture Stewart J Brown

Page 1: The face of coaching at the end of the 1950s - a Plaxton-bodied AEC Reliance.
Pages 2/3: An AEC Regal heads an impressive line-up of Wallace Arnold coaches in the late 1940s. The occasion - which involved 16 coaches capable of carrying almost 600 people - and the location have both been lost in the mists of time.

Published by
Bus Enthusiast Publishing Company
5 Hallcroft Close, Ratho, Newbridge
Midlothian EH28 8SD
Bus Enthusiast is an imprint of
Arthur Southern Ltd.

First published 1996
ISBN 0946265 22 4
© Bus Enthusiast Publishing Company, 1996
Typeset in Times and Helvetica
Electronic page makeup by Jeremy Scott
Printed by Pillans & Wilson, Edinburgh

Foreword

*by Malcolm Barr, Life President, Barr &
Wallace Arnold Trust*

MY FATHER ROBERT BARR was an idealist - but
one of that rare breed that also has great
practical ability and perseverance. Coming from
farming stock he was a country man at heart,
and it was this love of the country which urged
him to help town dwellers enrich their lives by
getting out into the country to enjoy its beauty
and freshness.

Writing in his book, *I travel the road*, he
said:

"It was in 1912 that I commenced with my
first motor coach, which I drove myself. I used
to pull up by the roadside to describe the
scenery. There were times we visited the old
Abbeys like Bolton and Rievaulx, Jervaulx,
Fountains and Kirkham. Although they were
ruins they always seem fitting memorials of a
bygone age. I found a great deal of pleasure and
delight in the response of the people I took on
these first excursions into the country."

I have no doubt at all that it was because
Robert Barr ran his company with the clear
ideal of giving public service that Wallace
Arnold has lasted long enough to justify a
history - and a history which has perforce
become just as much a chronicle of social
change, of customer service and therefore of a
wider general interest, which turns Stewart
Brown's work into a fascinating and important
contribution not just for Wallace Arnold, but for
the development of coaching in Britain and of
the coaches themselves.

Mr Brown has catalogued with great care
the 43 acquisitions made by Wallace Arnold
over the years and absorbed into that company;
these acquisitions were made in pursuit of a
clearly defined strategy - namely for Wallace
Arnold to become firstly the most significant
coach business in Yorkshire and later, as events
unfolded, in Great Britain as a whole.

This foreword would be incomplete without
a fuller acknowledgement of the unique part
played by Robert Barr in the company's success
and development. Robert Barr never lost his
philosophy of practical idealism, his love of
giving service to customers, his ambition to
succeed and his life long practice of fair dealing
with customers, staff and suppliers. He had a
zest for living which he infected on all those
fortunate enough to work with him.

Perhaps the next most significant
contributor to the company over the years was
Margaret Hook, Robert Barr's daughter, who
was appointed to the company in 1947 and
continued in one capacity or another for over 40
years. Very shortly after joining my father in
the business Margot became tours director and
was entirely responsible for activating the
immense post-war growth in passenger
carryings. She was a tireless worker, possessed
immense powers of application and a mind
fertile with ideas.

Margot brought drive and the
implementation of ambitious plans for the
growth of the business at precisely the time
when that growth was possible and sustainable.
On that aspect of the business primarily
concerned with the operation of the coach fleet
my brother Stuart Barr, Robert Barr's younger
son, made a significant contribution over many
years and not least of his many achievements
was the introduction of the now famous new
livery giving the very bold WA insignia a full
display.

Stewart Brown is to be congratulated on
creating an inspiring chronicle which does full
justice to its intensely interesting subject. This
book will certainly be fascinating to the
specialist coaching cognoscenti, especially
those interested in the development and uses of
passenger/commercial vehicles, but it also has
to have a very great interest for a wider
audience of general readers interested in the
development of this unique company and also
interested in the extraordinary development of
package tours during this 20th century.

I have been proud to be associated with
Wallace Arnold and cherish its traditions and its
progress. Unhesitatingly I give my very best
wishes to those who work for the company now
and in the future.

The formative years

The Bridge Garage, at which Robert Barr served his apprenticeship, operated this well-laden charabanc before World War I.

WALLACE ARNOLD TOURS is one of Britain's leading holiday coach tour businesses, carrying hundreds of thousands of people each year to destinations throughout Britain and Europe. Its coach fleet is one of Europe's most modern. But its roots can be traced back as far as 1912 when Robert Barr bought his first vehicle, a Karrier which operated as a lorry in Leeds during the week and as a charabanc for country trips at weekends.

Robert Barr's business grew slowly. Progress was halted when war broke out but recommenced as soon as peace returned. In 1920 he ran his first charabanc trip to London, no mean feat in the days of unsophisticated vehicles with solid tyres - and a trial for the passengers as well as the charabanc in the days when 12mph was the legal maximum speed and frequent stops had to be made to keep the engine topped up with water.

In 1926 Robert Barr took over the partnership of Wallace Cunningham and Arnold Crowe, Leeds charabanc operators, for the sum of £800. This was the springboard for expansion. Arnold Crowe left to pursue other interests but Wallace Cunningham stayed on until his death in 1950. The Wallace Arnold name was used by Robert Barr for his coaching activities while the haulage business developed as R Barr (Leeds) Ltd.

Wallace Arnold had been another pioneer in the provision of holiday coach tours from Leeds and in the summer of 1922 was advertising five days in London or in Edinburgh for £8 8s (£8.40) and a nine-day tour to the Scottish Highlands for 16 guineas (£16.80).

The days of the open charabanc were drawing to a close and the last survivor was withdrawn in 1928, by which time the company was running 15 purpose-built "all weather" coaches - so called because they had totally-enclosed bodywork. With these Wallace Arnold was running day trips to the coast and the Yorkshire Dales, as well as holiday coach tours to Devon, Scotland and Wales. A daily coach service at 9.30am from Leeds to Blackpool was offered in the early 1930s.

From 1927 all new coaches delivered to Wallace Arnold had pneumatic tyres, giving travellers a much smoother and quieter ride. Vehicles with pneumatic tyres also benefited from a relaxation in the outdated speed limit still in force in 1928, which was raised from 12mph to 20mph. The lower limit remained for solid-tyred vehicles.

Having built up a fleet of reliable coaches - mostly Leylands - the company set its sights further afield and in 1933 operated the first continental coach holiday from Yorkshire. The destination was Germany and the coach had to be hoisted on and off the ship. Drive-through car ferries for crossings to Europe were far in the future. The German coach holidays, including a Rhine cruise, were for 9 or 16 days and in 1936 an agreement was reached with an operator in Cologne who provided a coach for

Motor Show - London
We have been asked by many of our Patrons if we will run a Special 5 day Tour to London in connection with the above. Having secured for this occasion (at somewhat heavy cost) a Super Motor Coach, absolutely covered in and giving perfect protection, no matter what the weather conditions, we have decided to run a Tour on Monday, November 7th for 5 days, and would like to give you an opportunity of joining our party. There is only seating accommodation for 22, however, so we shall esteem it a favour if you will kindly advise us as early as possible, number of seats you would like us to reserve for you. *letter dated 31 October 1921 from Wallace Cunningham to a Mr Barker*

The first bus in the fleet, in 1919, was this 28-seat solid-tyred Karrier with the monogram RB over the rear wheels. This substantial-looking bus weighed only four tons unladen

the continental part of the trip, thus saving Wallace Arnold the cost and inconvenience of transporting vehicles across the North Sea.

Air travel was growing gradually in the 1930s and from 1935 Wallace Arnold acted as the West Yorkshire agent for a service connecting London, Leeds and Newcastle which was being operated by North Eastern Airways.

Wallace Arnold consolidated its position as one of the leading coach operators in the Leeds area by acquiring other smaller business. In the mid-1930s Harrison of Leeds, Fish of Morley and North of Bradford were taken over. Where acquired businesses had established a local reputation Wallace Arnold retained the company's name. Thus a new AEC Regal coach in 1933 operated with the Harrison name and a pair of new Maudslays in 1936 were run as Fish vehicles.

In 1937 Robert Barr formed a public company, the Barr & Wallace Arnold Trust Ltd. This took over his transport interests - R Barr (Leeds) Ltd, Wallace Arnold Tours Ltd, W H Fish & Son Ltd and Alf Harrison (Leeds) Ltd.

To extend the working lives of its vehicles Wallace Arnold started a limited programme of rebodying in 1937, sending reconditioned Leyland Tiger chassis to Duple in Hendon, north London. The first to be so treated were a pair of 1930 TS2s, followed in 1938 by a similar 1929 vehicle. Two TS4s were rebodied by Duple in 1940.

Car ownership was low in the 1930s and travel by touring coach was a luxury for the comparatively well-off. Wallace Arnold's tours, complete with courier and travelling rugs, were run by expensive vehicles stopping at exclusive hotels. It took postwar mass production to bring costs down and open up the coach holiday

market to a wider audience.

In 1930 the Wallace Arnold coach fleet numbered 15 vehicles; by the end of the decade this figure had more than doubled to 40. The R Barr haulage business had done well too. The fleet had grown as the increased reliability of lorries made long-distance running, in competition with the railways, a viable business proposition. When war broke out R Barr had a fleet of trucks carrying a wide range of products throughout Yorkshire, south to London, and across the taxing Pennine hills to Lancashire.

The delivery of new coaches came to a halt in 1940 as leisure travel gave way to essential traffic. The new coaches in 1940 were petrol-engined Leyland Tigers. Although diesel engines offered many advantages, not least in terms of operating economy, a small number of coach operators in the late 1930s stayed loyal to the smoother-running petrol engine to give their

In the early days Robert Barr operated lorries. The lettering on the side of this Karrier reads 'R Barr, Char-a-banc & Haulage Contractor'.

passengers a quiet, smooth ride. The 1940 Tigers were Wallace Arnold's last petrol-engined Leylands. They were converted to diesel power in 1947.

To aid the war effort the government requisitioned a dozen of the company's coaches in 1939-40 for use as ambulances and troop carriers. However Wallace Arnold was also helping the war effort locally by running services to Royal Ordnance and other factories, including the Avro factory at Yeadon. To do this it acquired a collection of fairly modern secondhand coaches from other operators in Yorkshire and Lancashire. Some were short-lived, but others were rebuilt after the war with new diesel engines and new coach bodies and pressed into service on the company's tours. The first double-deck bus in the fleet arrived in 1942 - a 13-year-old Leyland Titan TD1. Double-deck buses were to play a small part in the company's operations until 1972.

This Duple-bodied Leyland Tiger TS8 was the last word in luxury in the late 1930s. It had a smooth and silent six-cylinder petrol engine and 32-seat bodywork by Duple of London. The starting handle required a hefty swing.
Leyland

Operators taken over 1933-1944		
Year	**Operator**	**No of vehicles**
1933	W Fish, Morley	3
1933	Alf Harrison Ltd, Leeds	2
1936	J W North & Sons Ltd, Bradford	6
1937	G W Gayton, Bradford	-
1938	Smith Brothers and Co, Eccleshill	3
1938	S Crossley & Sons (Leeds) Ltd	2
1939	J North, Bradford	1
1939	J Cole & Sons (Leeds) Ltd	2
1939	W Robinson, Leeds	-
1940	H Sykes, Bradford	1
1940	F & H Croft, Yeadon	1
1941	H Walker, Leeds	1
1941	G R Townend & Son, Leeds	1
1941	G E Bilham, Royston	2

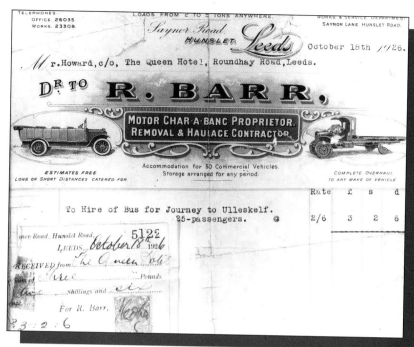

This 1928 advert publicises daily haulage services from Leeds carrying loads from one to 15 tons and the largest fleet of all-weather coaches in the district, catering for parties from 14 to 1,000. The coach illustrated is one of two new Albions.

A 1926 invoice for a trip to Ulleskelf which costs £3 2s 6d (£3.12). Other services offered include vehicle storage, with room for up to 50 commercial vehicles and overhauls. The haulage part of the business catered for loads from two to five tons.

This fine Albion PNA26 with roll-back canvas roof was one of six coaches delivered in 1928 and had seats for 26 passengers. The other 1928 deliveries comprised another similar Albion, two Tilling-Stevens, a Dennis and a Leyland Lion. This coach - petrol-engined as were all coaches at this time - was sold in 1930.
R L Grieves collection

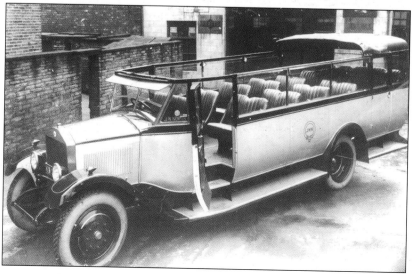

A contemporary of the Wallace Arnold Albion, this rakish Lancia was operated by North of Bradford whose business was taken over by Wallace Arnold in 1936. The canvas roof is rolled back to show the leather-covered seats. Interior lighting is provided by small lamps at the top of each window pillar.

The grand tour, 1930s style. Passengers on a Bournemouth holiday display the styles of the times. All but one wears a hat and the bare-headed gent has a winged collar.

Coach design advanced quite dramatically around 1930, and by 1933 coaches looked altogether more modern. This AEC Regal was one of a pair delivered to North of Bradford in 1933; and is seen later in the decade after North's business was taken over by Wallace Arnold. Compared with the coach in the previous picture the 30-seat body now had a solid roof with a centre section which slid open like the sunroof on a car, and a large luggage rack towards the rear. This coach gave the company remarkably long service. It was requisitioned by the Ministry of Supply during World War II and returned to Wallace Arnold in 1947 when it was rebodied - twice - before being sold in 1952. *W J Haynes*

This Leyland Tiger TS8 with 32-seat Duple bodywork is typical of the coaches being supplied to Wallace Arnold in the late 1930s. Ten were purchased between 1938 and 1940. After much rebuilding, re-engining and rebodying, most survived until the early 1950s. *Duple*

All aboard for the Leeds Mercury escorted motor tour. The year is 1937; the coach is a brand-new Duple-bodied Leyland Tiger. Robert Barr stands on the right; the coach driver attired in white dust coat leans proprietorially against the front wing. The name board above the side windows was illuminated at night. Observe the lady with the large hat box in the centre. The Leeds Mercury is no more and this coach had a short life; it was requisitioned by the Air Force in 1939, never to return to Leeds.

After the war

THE WAR ENDED IN 1945. The first new postwar Wallace Arnold coaches were on the road in the summer of 1946. There were four - an AEC Regal and a Leyland Tiger with bodies by Duple; a Plaxton-bodied Bedford OB, and a second Leyland Tiger with bodywork by Wilks & Meade.

Wilks & Meade, with a coachbuilding operation in Millwright Street, Leeds, had been acquired by Wallace Arnold in 1942. The plan was that with substantial in-house coachbuilding skills the company would be well-placed to rebuild its fleet as soon as the war was over - which is precisely what Wilks & Meade did, in an extensive programme between 1946 and the early 1950s. At its peak it employed 250 people.

The fleet's new AECs and Leylands looked little different from prewar coaches - but under the bonnet there was now a diesel engine. Thirsty petrol engines, no matter how smooth and quiet, were a luxury which could no longer be afforded in full-sized coaches in austere postwar Britain. The new Bedford delivered in 1946 had been ordered by Box of Castleford who were taken over by Wallace Arnold in August. One of the major attractions of the Box business was that four of its five coaches were brand new AEC Regals - at a time when new coaches were hard to come by.

With the four genuine new coaches came a pseudo-new coach, a 1932 Leyland Tiger TS4 acquired from a Leeds dealer in 1939 and operated as a lorry in the Barr haulage fleet until 1946 when it was fitted with a new Wilks & Meade coach body. The company was no stranger to rebuilding vehicles. It had had some elderly Leylands rebodied by Duple in the late 1930s and during the war it became involved in chassis rebuilding, creating 'new' chassis from acquired parts.

However this was but a prelude to a period of feverish activity in the late 1940s and early 1950s which saw an unprecedented programme of vehicle rebuilding and modernisation. The simplest part of what was a very complicated programme was the conversion of prewar petrol-engined coaches to diesel power and around 50 were undertaken between 1946 and 1950, often in association with other major work on the vehicle.

Most of the coaches converted were Leylands, which were fitted with either Leyland's prewar 8.6-litre diesel or the lighter postwar 7.4-litre unit. A small number of acquired prewar Leylands (five) were converted from 8.6 to 7.4 engines. Also treated were seven prewar AECs which were fitted with AEC's 7.7-litre diesel engine, and a pair of acquired Albions which also received AEC

There was a pent-up demand for travel in Britain when the war ended, as this queue outside the Leeds Corn Exchange in 1946 graphically illustrates. They were waiting to book on Wallace Arnold coastal express services. The panoramic picture is in fact a clever composite of three individual views carefully joined together.

These coaches are fine examples of the company's postwar rebuilds of prewar vehicles. On the left is an ex-North of Bradford Leyland Lion LT5A of 1934 with a 1944 Burlingham bus body, rebuilt as a 33-seat coach by Wilks & Meade in 1949 at which time its original petrol engine was replaced by a Leyland 7.4-litre diesel. On the right is a 1937 TS7 Tiger, one of three purchased in 1951 from a Leeds dealer. Before entering Wallace Arnold service it was fitted with the body shown, ostensibly a 1930 Brush body which was rebuilt by Wilks & Meade in 1949 and which came from a TS2 Tiger. It also received a Leyland 8.6-litre diesel engine from the same bus. It ran for two seasons, being sold at the end of 1952. Interestingly the rebuild on the left retained its original Bradford registration number while that on the right carried a new Leeds registration mark. *R F Mack*

diesel engines. The re-powering work grew to a peak - of 19 coaches - in 1949. The last few prewar coaches - all extensively rebuilt and fitted with new bodies after the war - were withdrawn in 1954.

The rebuilding of prewar coaches in the 1940s generally involved Wilks & Meade who either supplied completely new bodies, which they did for 10 coaches, or extensively rebuilt the existing bodywork which happened to another 30 vehicles. The rebuilding was frequently so comprehensive that little other than the frame was left of the original body.

In 1945 Wallace Arnold had made its first acquisitions outside the West Riding of Yorkshire. Four small coach operators were purchased in Scarborough - Barker, Queen's Motors, Fletcher's and Pullman Motors. This gave Wallace Arnold a foothold in a popular holiday destination. Between them the companies only owned four coaches but anticipating pent-up demand for coastal holidays Wallace Arnold allocated 12 new Bedford OBs to its Scarborough operation in 1947. The Scarborough fleet traded as Barker's until 1949 when it became part of the main Wallace Arnold operation.

The move into Scarborough was echoed two years later in Devon, when the operations of Waverley Coach Tours of Paignton were acquired in the summer of 1947. In the classic tradition of the seaside excursion operator Waverley owned two small Bedford coaches which dated from the mid-1930s. They were promptly replaced by four new Bedford OBs which were operated under the Waverley name.

Another Paignton operator, Ruby Tours with seven Bedford coaches, was taken over in 1949.

Three of the Bedfords were prewar models and were quickly replaced by two new Bedfords and a Leyland Tiger. Another two new coaches, a Daimler CVD6 and a further Bedford, swelled the Ruby fleet to nine vehicles. Ruby operated holiday coach tours which included a seven-day tour to Blackpool for the Illuminations. As with Waverley, the goodwill associated with the Ruby Tours business led to the name being retained for most of the following decade. Ultimately a combined Ruby and Waverley Tours excursion brochure was produced, but the only mention of the parent company was the legend "associated with Wallace Arnold Tours" on the back page.

The company's interest in Devon - a key prewar holiday destination - had been re-affirmed in 1945 with the purchase of two adjacent hotels in Torquay, Oswalds and the Trecarn, both still owned and used by the company's coach tours.

New additions to the fleet in the late 1940s were quite a mixture. Demand for transport outstripped supply. Those who could afford new cars had to join a two-year waiting list. Coach travel reached new heights of popularity. And coach operators generally bought whatever vehicles were available quickly. Wallace Arnold standardised on the petrol-engined Bedford OB for operations which needed a small vehicle; 34 were purchased between 1946 and 1950. OBs were allocated to the newly-acquired excursion fleets in Scarborough and Paignton, as well as being used on tours from Yorkshire where narrow roads precluded the use of full-size coaches.

Not that the full-sized coaches of the 1940s were much bigger than the Bedfords. The OB

Another vehicle with a complex history was this 1933 Leyland Tiger TS4 which operated as a coach until 1939 when it was converted to a lorry and transferred to the R Barr haulage operation. After six months as a lorry it was sent to Duple for a new coach body and re-entered service with Wallace Arnold in 1940. In 1946 it was fitted with a diesel engine and in 1949 its body was rebuilt by Wilks & Meade. It is seen here in 1952, shortly before being withdrawn, operating on the Farsley Omnibus Co's service at Rodley. *R F Mack*

This 1930 Leyland Tiger TS2 joined the Wallace Arnold fleet in 1941 when the company was extending its wartime operations carrying workers to factories in and around Leeds. It was rebuilt as shown here in 1950, carrying a late prewar Duple 33-seat coach body and fitted with a diesel engine. It was sold after one season's touring in this form. The deep radiator was a postwar fitment designed to make the ageing Tiger look more modern. When new it would have had a much shallower radiator. *R F Mack*

was a 29-seater; the standard big coach of the time seated only 33. Most of Wallace Arnold's new coaches in the late 1930s had been Leylands, and this make predominated in the early postwar years. Between 1946 and 1949 the company bought 37 PS1 Tigers, followed by 11 of the bigger-engined PS2 model in 1949-50. This total of 48 Leylands compares with 24 AECs, 10 Daimlers and a solitary Guy supplied over the same period. Most of the bodies for these coaches came from three suppliers - Duple in London, Burlingham in Blackpool, and Wilks & Meade. In all Wilks & Meade supplied the Wallace Arnold fleet with 40 coach bodies on new or reconditioned chassis between 1946 and 1950, as well as supplying small numbers of bodies to other operators.

By 1948 Wallace Arnold could boast offices in ten northern towns and cities, plus what it called its London office - which was actually in Croydon. It had agents in 23 towns, some of which were other well-known bus and coach operators: Premier Travel in Cambridge, Hansons Buses in Huddersfield and Hall Bros in South Shields. The Thomas Cook organisation was an authorised Wallace Arnold agent in Leeds, Hull, Sheffield and York.

Tour departures - up to 21 a week - were being offered from Leeds, Scarborough, Bridlington and Hull and patrons were being enticed to "see beautiful Britain from a cosy armchair" at prices from 12 guineas (£12.60) for six days in the Wye Valley and Wales to £19 10s (£19.50) for nine days in the North West Highlands (based in Oban and Inverness) or ten days in Devon and Cornwall. For the adventurous (and well-off) a 14-day tour to Switzerland - the only foreign tour available - cost £51. In 1949 additional continental tours were being offered to the French and Italian Rivieras (17 days for £66) and to Holland (nine days for £36). The programme was further expanded in 1950.

The early postwar period saw the reintroduction of a daily express service from Leeds to Blackpool, along with daily summer services to Bridlington, Filey, Scarborough and Southport. Morecambe was served on bank holiday Saturdays, with a return journey the following Saturday.

Although essentially a Yorkshire company, Wallace Arnold had long recognised the potential of the market for foreign tourists arriving in London. The company's southern business received a significant boost in 1948 when it acquired the tours licences of Homeland Tours of Croydon, giving it a strong southern base on which to expand. Early postwar publicity aimed at the American market offered four tours from London with pick up points at the municipal car park in Croydon and Kings Cross Coach Station. In addition a "delightful selection of motor coach tours" from Yorkshire was offered to American clientele with rail travel from London to Leeds and overnight accommodation in Leeds before and after the tour. The company even produced brochures for North America with dollar prices. A 14-day tour of the Scottish Highlands - which actually got no further north than Aberdeen - cost $190 in 1949.

The haulage operation, R Barr (Leeds) Ltd, was nationalised in 1949, becoming part of the British Transport Commission's Road Haulage Executive - better known as British Road Services.

Coach number four on the Blackpool express on a sunny summer Saturday in 1950 was this 1937 Leyland Tiger TS7. It was purchased in 1941 and its Harrington body was rebuilt by Wilks & Meade in 1949, by which time it had acquired a Leyland 7.4-litre diesel engine. It ran as shown until 1953, when it was further modernised by the fitment of a 1947 Plaxton coach body. It was sold in 1954 and ended its days with an operator in Ireland in the early 1960s. *R F Mack*

Three vehicles were acquired with the business of Whitehead of Leeds in 1945. The oldest was this 1936 Albion Valkyrie PV141, seen after being rebodied by Wilks & Meade in 1949 and converted to diesel power using an AEC 7.7-litre engine. It was sold in 1952. The Wilks & Meade body had a strong resemblance to contemporary Duple bodywork. Albions were an unusual type in the Wallace Arnold Fleet. *R F Mack*

Box of Castleford, with four brand new AEC Regal coaches, was acquired in 1946. This Regal with 32-seat Plaxton body was an ex-Box coach and it ran with Wallace Arnold until 1955, by which time it was one of the last half-cab coaches in the fleet.
R Marshall

A tightly-packed line-up in Royston depot taken around 1948. From left to right are a 1944 Duple-bodied Bedford, one of 12 OWBs delivered to cover essential wartime bus services; a 1930 Leyland Tiger TS2 with Brush body, originally owned by Yorkshire Traction; a 1947 Burlingham-bodied Leyland Tiger PS1; and a 1937 Leyland Tiger TS7 acquired from Morecambe Motors in 1941.

Pudsey garage was photographed at around the same time and seems only marginally less tightly packed. Nearest the camera is a 1947 Leyland Tiger with Wilks & Meade body and alongside it a 1948 SMT-bodied Bedford OB. In the farther part of the garage there is a 1937 Leyland Tiger TS7 with Harrington body, acquired from Shaw of Warrington in 1941, and another 1948 OB with SMT body.

The postwar boom: passengers mill about among coaches at The Calls in April 1946. A prewar Leyland Tiger is visible in the centre background. The Bedford OWB to the left of the picture was not a Wallace Arnold vehicle.

No fewer than 22 new Leyland coaches joined the fleet in 1947. It was not until 1969 that Leyland again supplied as many coaches to the company in one year. This 1947 Tiger had a Plaxton body, one of the first bodies to be supplied to Wallace Arnold by the Scarborough-based coachbuilder. A radiator blind is fitted to improve the performance of the heaters. This coach was rebodied by Duple in 1953 and the Plaxton body transferred to a prewar Tiger.
M A Taylor

The 1946 Leeds registration mark and the 1948 Burlingham coach body conceal a 1933 AEC Regal which Wallace Arnold acquired from the Ministry of Supply at the end of World War II. The fitment of a 7.7-litre AEC diesel engine further hid its real age and it operated until 1954. It is seen on a football supporters hire at the Leeds United ground. The pantographs of eight Leeds trams awaiting the crowds at the end of the match are visible over the coach roofs. *R F Mack*

This 1937 Leyland Tiger TS7, originally owned by the West Riding Automobile Co of Wakefield, was purchased from a Leeds dealer in 1949. Its prewar bus body was scrapped and replaced with a prewar coach body. After four years operation it was then fitted with the body illustrated, a 1947 Burlingham coach body removed from a Leyland Tiger PS1 which was itself being rebodied as part of the company's modernisation programme. *J B Parkin*

This Leyland Tiger PS1 with Burlingham body was an early addition to the Ruby Tours fleet under Wallace Arnold's ownership. It was fitted with a radio and has a fine brass fire extinguisher, mounted on the pillar beside the door. Coaches were much lighter then than now; this one weighed just under 7 tons.

The Bedford OB played a significant role in early postwar coaching, serving on holiday coach tours and day trips. This 1948 OB with Duple Vista bodywork is seen awaiting excursionists at Scarborough in the early 1950s. It had originally been destined for a Wakefield operator - hence its West Riding registration instead of the customary Leeds mark. *R F Mack*

Smaller numbers of Leyland Tigers were purchased between 1948 and 1950. Six of those delivered in 1948 had 33-seat Duple bodies. This vehicle retained its original body, but was rebuilt with a full-width front in 1954. It was sold in 1958. *M A Taylor*

A promotional postcard produced by the company and carrying the address of Waverley Tours - although this 1947 Wilks & Meade-bodied Leyland Tiger PS1 was in fact a Wallace Arnold coach.

Operators acquired 1945-1949		
Year	**Operator**	**No of vehicles**
1945	T Whitehead & Sons (Motors) Ltd, Leeds	3
1945	G Barker (Scarborough) Ltd	1
1945	Fletcher's Coaches, Scarborough	-
1945	Pullman Motors, Scarborough	-
1945	Queen's Motors Ltd, Scarborough	3
1946	S Stone (Raglan Motors), Leeds	3
1946	L Leighton, Armley	1
1946	A E Aspinall, Pudsey	2
1946	M Box (Castleford) Ltd	5
1947	H G B Rawlings, Scarborough	3
1947	Waverley Motor Coach Tours Ltd, Paignton	2
1949	Ruby Tours Ltd, Paignton	7

Daimler coaches played a small part in Wallace Arnold's operations. Ten were bought between 1947 and 1949 and all were bodied by Wilks & Meade. The last of the ten is seen outside Blackpool's Coliseum coach station in 1953. Eight of the Daimlers, including this one, later received new double-deck bus bodies as shown on page 27. 1949 was the last year in which new half-cab coaches were purchased. *D Akrigg/R F Mack*

Before and after. Six Burlingham-bodied AEC Regal IIIs were delivered in 1949, five of which were fitted with new 8ft-wide Plaxton 35-seat coach bodies in 1952-53. The contrast in the appearance of the same coach before and after rebodying is quite remarkable. Before being rebodied the coach looked little different from those being operated in the 1930s. Coach design progressed quickly in the early 1950s and the new body with its full-width front and curved glass corner screens brought the coach right up to date.
D Akrigg/R F Mack

Craftsmen at work in Wilks & Meade. The three men in the foreground are all metal workers, cutting and shaping panels. In the left background a coachbuilder is trying a panel on a wooden framed coach rear end.

Boom years for coaching

BRITISH COACH DESIGN underwent its most radical change in 1950 with the launch of new underfloor-engined chassis from the two major manufacturers, AEC and Leyland. Gone was the vertical front engine and the separate driver's cab. Almost overnight the new coaches of the 1940s looked out of date.

Anticipating the trend towards the new models Wallace Arnold had in 1950 specified fully-fronted bodywork on conventional front-engined chassis. The full-width front offered no advantages. It added weight and it impeded access to the engine - but at least it looked modern, with the radiator concealed behind a stylish grille.

However the new coaches delivered in 1951 marked the start of a new era. They were bigger, built to the newly permitted maximum length of 30ft, and they seated 37 passengers - four more than the previous generation. A total of 13 underfloor-engined coaches entered Wallace Arnold service in 1951, ten Leyland Royal Tigers and three AEC Regal IVs. All had Burlingham's stylish new Seagull body with a centre entrance and a pair of seats up front alongside the driver offering two lucky passengers a grandstand view of the journey ahead.

It was also a period of change for Bedford, whose little normal control OB was replaced by the forward-control SB and four of these, with 33-seat Duple bodies, joined the Wallace Arnold fleet in 1951. At this time the livery was changed from summer ivory and carnation red to all over ivory. Bedford offered the option of a Perkins R6 diesel engine in the SB and Wallace Arnold tried one in 1954. However it was found to be excessively noisy and was fitted with a Bedford petrol engine in the spring of 1955. The last petrol-engined Bedfords were withdrawn from the fleet in 1959.

The extensive programme of conversions from petrol to diesel engines in the late 1940s was followed by a complicated series of body

This remarkable line-up, captioned 'Burlingham fleet 1954' on the original print, shows no fewer than 26 Burlingham Seagulls at the company's depot in Chadwick Street, off Hunslet Road in Leeds.

transfers and rebodying in the early 1950s. The transfers were carried out using tram jacks to lift and support the old body. The chassis was then rolled out and renovated before being fitted with a new body. Meanwhile the old body was left standing on oil drums while awaiting transfer to an even older chassis whose body was scrapped.

The rebodying of prewar chassis in the late 1940s was followed by rebodying of early postwar chassis from 1951. By 1954 a total of 25 postwar chassis had been fitted with new fully-fronted bodies and a further 35 coaches had new full-width fronts grafted on to their old half-cab bodies. Much of this work was done by Wilks & Meade using parts supplied by coachbuilders Yeates of Loughborough and Plaxton of Scarborough. On top of all that some 56 body transfers were carried out between 1949 and 1954. The net result of this activity was a continual updating of the fleet.

The last Wallace Arnold half-cab coach was withdrawn in 1955. The new generation of coach chassis from AEC and Leyland was considerably heavier than their predecessors - sometimes by almost a ton. The Leyland Royal Tigers had vacuum brakes which were barely up to the job of stopping a fully-laden coach weighing around 11 tons and in the winter of 1953-54 the ten delivered in 1951 plus eight purchased in 1952 were converted to air brakes with much improved performance. Learning from experience, the Royal Tigers delivered to Wallace Arnold in 1953 had air brakes from the outset.

Leylands still outnumbered AECs, but the balance swung the other way from 1954 when the original heavyweight underfloor-engined chassis were replaced by new lighter models -

1950s modernity in Leeds booking office. The picture is easily dated as 1953 by the coronation poster above the counter clerk on the right. The clerk points to a spot in Ireland as he outlines the route of a tour to a potential holidaymaker. The glass brick counter facia seems surprisingly modern.

AEC's Reliance and Leyland's Tiger Cub. The Tiger Cub had a two-speed rear axle which some drivers found difficult to master and which was also unreliable. The axles were soon locked in high ratio. The Reliance was seen as a better chassis, although it later developed a poor reputation for cooling system problems. Thus in 1954 AEC supplied 20 Reliances while only two Leyland Tiger Cubs were purchased. In 1955 no Leylands were bought at all and from then until the early 1960s - by which time Leyland had taken over AEC - AECs outnumbered Leylands in Wallace Arnold's new coach programme. The Tiger Cubs and Reliances turned in remarkable fuel economy with figures of up to 15.4mpg being recorded by the company on its holiday tours.

Bedford's leadership of the lighter end of the coach market was challenged in the early 1950s by Commer, with the forward-control Avenger model. Three Avengers were purchased by Wallace Arnold in 1952 and small repeat orders were placed between 1954 and 1957. The Commers had front-mounted two-stroke diesel engines which tended to be noisy. After buying a total of 17 Commers, Wallace Arnold purchased one Bedford, an SB1, in 1959. For comparison the company also took delivery of an example of Ford's new 570E coach chassis, a front-engined lightweight designed to compete head-on with the Bedford SB. The Ford was one of four vehicles hired from Stanley Hughes, the Cleckheaton coach dealer, and was only operated for one summer season.

The hiring of new coaches was in itself a significant departure from established practice. Wallace Arnold had on occasion hired used coaches from Stanley Hughes to cover short summer peaks but the hiring of new vehicles, which were returned to the dealer for resale after only a few months use, was innovative.

At the start of the 1950s Wallace Arnold was offering eight continental tours to Switzerland, France, Austria, Italy, Holland and Spain and ranging in price from 35 to 57 guineas (£36.75 to £59.85). Two of the tours offered only one departure each year, but others operated up to nine times in a season.

The 1950s were the golden days of coach excursions. Car ownership was still low - but rising - and licensing by the traffic commissioners kept tight control over which companies could operate coach excursions, the destinations they could serve, and the fares they could charge. Both Leeds and Bradford had extensive excursion programmes catering for travel-hungry workers. In Leeds Wallace Arnold vied with Heaps and West Yorkshire for custom, while in Bradford there were five licensed operators - Wallace Arnold, Wardways, Feather Bros, Ledgard and West Yorkshire. The positioning of coaches on the Bradford pick-up stand each day was determined by a draw. The central starting points in Leeds and Bradford were augmented by suburban pick-up points on the main routes out of each city.

The company's position as an excursion operator in Scarborough was consolidated in March 1952 with the acquisition of the Hardwick's business. Hardwick's ran 14 vehicles, mostly Bedfords, and operated local bus services in the area, running to Ebberston and, on Saturdays, to Malton. The six oldest Hardwick's vehicles were sold immediately without being replaced as Wallace Arnold rationalised its operations in the town. But the local bus services were sufficiently busy for Wallace Arnold to order a new double-deck bus for the first time in its history - a Leyland Titan PD2 which was delivered in 1953. A similar vehicle followed in 1954; both had Leyland bodywork. The Hardwick's name was retained by Wallace Arnold until the company sold its Scarborough operations to the EYMS Group in 1987.

A wide range of day tours was operated from Scarborough in the early 1950s under the Wallace Arnold banner with prices ranging from 1s 3d (6p) for a short circular tour of Scarborough and Oliver's Mount, to 13s (65p) for a day to Stokesley and the Cleveland Hills.

In October 1952 the company's bus-operating interests were expanded with the purchase of the tiny Farsley Omnibus Co of Stanningley, on the outskirts of Leeds. Farsley operated four reasonably new Daimler CVD6 single-deckers on

a route from Pudsey town centre to Horsforth. The Daimlers continued to operate the Farsley services until the fleet was re-equipped in 1956-57 when eight of the Daimler coaches purchased by Wallace Arnold in the late 1940s were fitted with new 61-seat double-deck bus bodies by Charles H Roe, whose works were in Crossgates on the eastern edge of Leeds. Six of these were allocated to the Farsley fleet. In 1959 Farsley's services carried 2.3 million passengers.

Service Motors of Leeds was purchased in 1954 for their contracts, which included one to a car auction site at Measham.

Tours to Northern and Southern Ireland appeared in 1954, when the company was still appealing to the dollar market with a brochure which showed prices in dollars and in sterling. By 1955 Wallace Arnold claimed to be carrying over 25,000 tour passengers a year. It also claimed to be running a fleet of over 250 coaches - which was just a bit of an exaggeration. The real figure was nearer 200.

In this year it became one of the first British coach tour operators to provide low-priced off-season holidays for elderly people, opening up a market which was to grow dramatically. A savings club was operated in the 1950s which encouraged customers to buy stamps in denominations of 1s, 2s 6d, or 5s (5p, 12p or 25p) which could be used in part payment for tickets on express services, excursions or extended tours.

Major expansion came in March 1955 with the acquisition of the business of Feather Brothers of Bradford. Feathers operated a modern fleet; its oldest coaches were four 1950 Dennis Lancets which were retained by Wallace Arnold for the 1955 season and sold at the start of 1956. Feathers operated a low-price holiday tour programme, Cresta Tours, and was one of the first providers of specially-priced holidays for elderly people - for which would-be customers had to produce their pension books. In 1958 a seven day holiday by Feathers to Eastbourne for elderly travellers cost only £9 10s (£9.50) in

A pair of Bedford OBs pause for a picture on a children's outing in 1950. Both have Duple Vista bodies. The coach on the left was new in 1949; that on the right in 1947. Wallace Arnold bought 34 of these attractive petrol-engined coaches between 1946 and 1950.

Second-hand double-deckers played a part in the company's contract and local bus operations in the 1940s and early 1950s. This Roe-bodied Leyland Titan TD4 came from Leeds City Transport in 1950. It dated back to 1936 and served Wallace Arnold until the end of 1956.

April, May, September and October. By contrast the peak season Cresta tour to the same resort cost 17½ guineas (£18.38) The Feathers name was retained until the early 1970s.

In 1954 Wallace Arnold made a move across the Pennines with a view to building up its business in Lancashire. It took over the extended tours business of Yelloway of Rochdale and started running tours from Lancashire amid strong opposition from local operators. The opposition was such that Wallace Arnold's licences carried severe restrictions and direct operation from Lancashire was quietly abandoned in 1958.

There was diversification in 1955. The demand for travel had grown dramatically in the 10 years since the end of World War II, but it was clear that with it there was a growing demand for private transport which could undermine the company's main business. Aware of this, the Barr & Wallace Arnold Trust moved into vehicle sales.

Its first franchise was to sell Sentinel trucks and coaches. Wallace Arnold Sales & Service was formed in 1955 and supplied Sentinel lorries and four SLC6 coaches to Schofield of Marsden. One SLC6, with Burlingham Seagull body, was also delivered to the Wallace Arnold operating fleet and ran from 1955 to 1962. Sentinel's great days had passed, and Wallace Arnold Sales & Service quickly relinquished the franchise - but not before it had learned enough to briefly become Rootes Group dealers before settling down with a Nuffield Group franchise which covered Morris, Morris Commercial, Wolseley and MG.

A new car showroom in Hunslet Road, Leeds, was opened by Lord Brabazon of Tara, chairman of Associated Commercial Vehicles, in 1958. The Hunslet Road premises covered almost 100,000 sq ft and its plate glass windows were amongst the biggest in Leeds. WASS expanded, acquiring the Vauxhall and Bedford franchises, and was later joined by Trust Motors, initially selling Volkswagens. Both companies continue as part of the Barr & Wallace Arnold Trust organisation.

Further expansion of the company's local bus operating interests in the Leeds area came in June 1956 with the purchase of Kippax & District. This company ran two single-deck and four double-deck buses, three of which were 20 years old, on a service from Leeds Central Bus Station to Kippax and Garforth. In 1959 Kippax & District, now running six double-deck buses, was carrying 1.4 million passengers.

Consolidation in Devon came in 1956-57 with the takeover of three Torquay operators. Excelsior Coaches, Cream Cars and Sunbeam Garages ran 12 coaches between them, most of which were quickly disposed of by Wallace Arnold. The Cream Cars name was retained for a period. The company then reappraised its Devon operations and formed a new subsidiary, Wallace Arnold Tours (Devon) to control its interests in the south west of England.

A new coach station and car park was opened in Leeds city centre at The Calls in the summer of 1957. For this the company was praised by the chairman of the Yorkshire traffic commissioners who said that he welcomed any efforts by operators to help relieve the congestion caused by passenger vehicles standing in the centre of a city.

In the company's heartland Kitchin of Pudsey with 11 coaches was acquired in January 1959. Kitchin was primarily an excursion and hire operator. Most of the Kitchin coaches were modern enough to see a few seasons' service under Wallace Arnold ownership and two AEC Reliances which were less than 12 months old at the time of the takeover survived until 1967. The Kitchin name was retained until the late 1960s.

Express services were developed throughout the 1950s and by the end of the decade Wallace Arnold was operating a daily service from Leeds, Bradford and Huddersfield to Manchester's Ringway Airport. There was also a daily service to Blackpool - which in the winter was operated jointly with the nationalised West Yorkshire Road Car Company. Summer season express services included a daily link between Leeds and Scarborough, Filey and Bridlington; and once-a-week services from Leeds to Morecambe, Southport, Skegness, and Torquay and Paignton. A night service ran from Bradford, Castleford and Wakefield to Great Yarmouth. By 1959 express services were covering 300,000 miles a year and carrying 80,000 passengers.

The last of the popular Bedford OBs were delivered in 1950. By this time Wallace Arnold had 39 which included five acquired from other operators. One of the last OBs is hoisted aboard a ferry bound for Holland on one of the company's growing list of continental holiday tours.

The first of the new generation of underfloor-engined coaches entered service in 1951. Ten were Leyland Royal Tigers with Burlingham Seagull bodies. They were 37-seaters at a time when most operators were fitting 41 seats in coaches of this size. These vehicles ran with Wallace Arnold until 1960.

The last front-engined AECs and Leylands were delivered in 1950 and had fully-fronted bodies. Pride of place in the 1950 deliveries went to this well-appointed Leyland Tiger PS2. Its Duple body had sumptuous two-and-one seating for only 21 passengers (compared with 33 on a conventional coach) and offered unparalleled comfort. It was shipped to New York and exhibited at the World Fair. Sliding roofs were still a common feature on touring coaches in 1950, but a glazed sliding roof was most unusual. This coach was soon upseated to 33 and eventually had its chassis lengthened and a new Plaxton body fitted in 1954. This was the first coach to be delivered in summer ivory livery with no red relief.

Not all of the early body designs for underfloor-engined chassis were as well-balanced as Burlingham's Seagull. This heavy-looking body came from Plaxton and was one of three delivered in 1952 on AEC Regal IV chassis. The heavily ornamented sidelight mouldings would not have looked out of place in an Odeon cinema. It is seen leaving Wembley Stadium on a private hire, followed by a Burlingham-bodied Regal IV from the Feathers fleet.
R H G Simpson

To add a touch of modernity to front-engined coaches Wallace Arnold instituted a programme of rebuilding them with full-width fronts. This 1948 AEC Regal III had its Duple body rebuilt by Yeates in 1952 with a full-width front and simplified side mouldings which included removal of a stylish, but old-fashioned, swoop behind the rear wheel arch. It is seen on a football supporters hire in Leeds in 1953 - but the destination blind serves as a reminder of grander trips.
D Akrigg/R F Mack

Operators acquired 1950-59		
Year	**Operator**	**No of vehicles**
1952	Hardwick's Motor Services Ltd, Scarborough	14
1952	Farsley Omnibus Co, Stanningley	4
1953	Devon Touring Co, Torquay	1
1953	J A Hudson (Leeds) Ltd	-
1954	Service Motors, Leeds	4
1955	Feather Brothers (Tours) Ltd, Bradford	16
1956	Kippax & District Motor Co Ltd	6
1957	Excelsior Coaches, Torquay	2
1958	Cream Cars, Torquay	8
1958	Sunbeam Garages, Torquay	2
1959	J W Kitchin & Sons Ltd, Pudsey	11

The first Duple bodies on Leyland Royal Tiger chassis were delivered in 1952. There were eight, one of which is seen outside the Feathers office in Bradford. The blackboards propped against the office offer tours to Scarborough and to the Blackpool Illuminations. A trip on the morning departure to Blackpool cost 11s 9d (59p); the afternoon departure was cheaper at 8s 3d (41p). *G Stainthorpe*

Above, left: In 1952 the Farsley Omnibus Co was taken over. It operated four Daimler CVD6 single-deck buses with 35-seat Roe bodies, new in 1947-48, three of which are seen lined up in Leeds in 1958. They had been replaced by double-deckers in 1956.

Above: Six Plaxton-bodied Bedford SBs were delivered in 1953. Two were allocated to the Ruby fleet in Devon, where this coach is seen. They were among the last petrol-engined coaches purchased and were operated until 1959. *J B Parkin*

This was Wallace Arnold's first new double-deck bus, a Leyland-bodied Titan PD2/12 delivered in 1953 for the Hardwick's operation in Scarborough. The advert on the side promotes trips to Forge Valley. The bus is seen in Leeds with a 1956 Plaxton-bodied AEC Reliance in the background. *J B Parkin*

Two different Burlingham bodies were carried by this 1947 Leyland Tiger. This is its second body, transferred in 1953 from a 1950 Tiger which was being rebodied by Plaxton. It is seen at Keadby Bridge, Scunthorpe in the summer of 1956.
D Akrigg/R F Mack

In 1954 Wallace Arnold sold this Leyland Tiger PS1 to the Ulster Transport Authority for exclusive use on Wallace Arnold's Ulster tours. The chassis dated from 1947 but had a 1949 Burlingham body which had been transferred from an AEC Regal in 1952 and was then rebuilt with a Plaxton-style full-front by Wilks & Meade. It operated for four seasons with UTA.
R C Ludgate

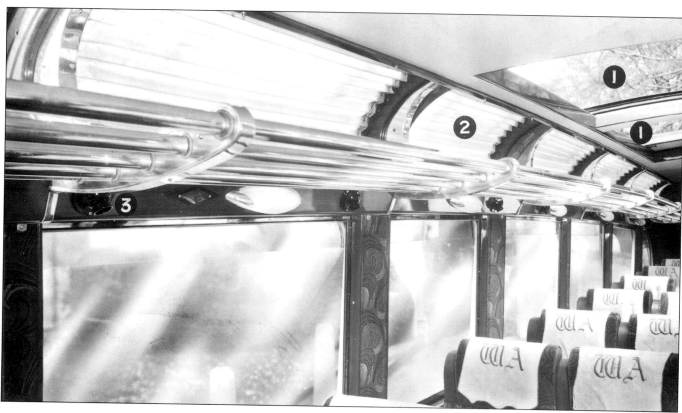

The interior of a Duple-bodied coach of 1952. Observe (1) the sliding sun roof to maximise your enjoyment of the sunshine and (2) the venetian blinds over the cove windows to ensure that the sun doesn't become too much of a nuisance. Fresh air was also provided by forced ventilation fed through nozzles (3) above the windows. Other period fittings are the antimacassars on each seat and the stylish lamp shades above the windows.

Surprising second-hand purchases in 1954 were three two-year old Plaxton-bodied AEC Regal IIIs. This was one of two which had been new to Morecambe Motors. It ran until 1956. In this 1955 view it is seen on a Gayways excursion. *R Marshall*

To swell the intake of new coaches in 1953 Wallace Arnold purchased two second-hand Leyland Tiger PS1s from Comberhill Motors, the Wakefield dealer. They had been new in 1948 to Longstaff of Mirfield and had 33-seat Burlingham bodies. Before entering service with Wallace Arnold they were sent to Plaxton to have modern-looking full-width cabs fitted. *R F Mack*

During the mid-1950s Wallace Arnold tried Commer chassis as an alternative to Bedford for its excursion fleet. This is an Avenger II, delivered in 1954 and photographed in Thirsk Market Place the following year. All of the Commers had Plaxton bodies. *D Akrigg*

Having been appointed sales agents for Sentinel trucks and buses Wallace Arnold added an SLC6 coach to its fleet. This had a Burlingham Seagull body and had been another exhibit at the 1954 Commercial Motor Show. It entered service in 1955. Sentinel never achieved great sales of buses and coaches and the only indication that this is in fact a fairly rare vehicle is the small Sentinel badge in the centre of the front grille. Power was provided by Sentinel's own 9.12-litre six-cylinder horizontal engine. Despite the fact that it was a non-standard vehicle, the Sentinel ran for Wallace Arnold until 1962. It is seen in Leeds at The Calls coach station. Cars in the 1s(5p)-a-day car park include a Standard Vanguard, an Austin Princess and a Hillman Husky estate car. Shell offered three grades of petrol in the days before star-ratings were invented - Shellmex, Shell and Super Shell.

The Tigers which were being rebodied looked like this, transformed from old-fashioned vehicles with exposed radiators, to modern-looking fully-fronted coaches. A Tiger with its new Plaxton body is seen posed on the seafront at Scarborough prior to delivery to Wallace Arnold. *Plaxton*

In 1955 Wallace Arnold took over the Feather Bros business in Bradford and with it came this new Dennis Lancet UF with 41-seat Yeates body. The Dennis had been an exhibit at the 1954 Commercial Motor Show at Earls Court but was not licensed for service until the spring of 1955, after Wallace Arnold had purchased Feathers. *R H G Simpson*

Until 1955 all of the company's underfloor-engined coaches had centre entrances. This standardisation was abandoned in 1956 with the delivery of seven Leyland Tiger Cubs and one AEC Reliance with front-entrance Burlingham Seagull bodywork which also had flat glass windscreens, introducing a saving in cost at the expense of style. *R H G Simpson*

Twelve coaches from the Devon fleet lined up in 1956. All have Plaxton bodies and most are Commers. Nearest the camera are 1956 Avenger IIIs WUG395-399, followed by identical 1954 coaches UUB400-404, all neatly parked in numerical order. The last two vehicles are Bedford SBs of 1953 and 1954 vintage respectively.

Smile please. Smartly-dressed holidaymakers pause for a picture on a Feathers tour to the West Country. The coach is a 1956 Commer. *M Elphee*

Proving that there's nothing new under the sun, this Burlingham-bodied AEC Reliance of 1957 demonstrates an early form of continental exit - a feature which British coach operators were to re-invent 25 years later. The emergency door opens to reveal steps which can be used by passengers entering or leaving the coach while on the continent. This allows them to step on to the pavement instead of having to risk life and limb by stepping out into the traffic.

Kippax & District was acquired by Wallace Arnold in June 1956. The newest buses in the fleet were two 1948 Leyland Titan PD2s with 56-seat Leyland bodies. Advertising for Wilks & Meade is carried on the side of this bus in Leeds Central Bus Station. *A D Broughall*

Kitchin of Pudsey was taken over in 1959. No fewer than six of its 11 vehicles were less than a year old, including this Plaxton-bodied AEC Reliance which was kept by Wallace Arnold until 1967. The coach alongside is a 1958 Bristol LS6B belonging to United Automobile Services of Darlington. *G Stainthorpe*

In 1956-57 eight Daimler CVD6 coaches dating from 1948-49 were fitted with new 61-seat double-deck bus bodies by Charles H Roe of Crossgates, Leeds. The eight vehicles were allocated to each of Wallace Arnold's three bus operations - Farsley Omnibus Co, Hardwick's and Kippax Motors. A family complete with collapsible push chair board a Farsley bus at Stanningley Bottom.

A 1956 Commer Avenger III posed at Haytor Rock on the Widdicombe road on Dartmoor. It has Plaxton bodywork. This was Commer's best year with Wallace Arnold, when it supplied seven coaches - four for Ruby, one for Waverley and two to the Feathers fleet in Bradford. The Commers generally lasted five years with Wallace Arnold.

Below, left: The 1959 coaches included some of the first examples of Plaxton's trend-setting Panorama design. This had three long windows to give passengers an uninterrupted view of the scenery outside. The windows were sealed, with ventilation being provided by a scoop on the roof which forced air into the saloon. Venetian blinds - just visible in this photograph - could be lowered when the sun got hot, which it doubtless did on this tour to Spain. *J B Parkin*

Below: This odd vehicle was a 1953 Plaxton-bodied AEC Regal IV which had lain unsold in the stock of Hughes, the Cleckheaton coach dealer, until being purchased by Wallace Arnold - doubtless at an extremely attractive price - in 1957. It ran until 1965. It was also the first coach in the fleet to have a reversed registration with the numbers preceding the letters. Leeds was one of only four licensing authorities to issue reversed registrations with a single index letter. *R H G Simpson*

The late 1950s were good years for AEC at Wallace Arnold. A total of 71 Reliances was purchased between 1958 and 1960. The 1959 delivery comprised 24 coaches, 18 of which had Plaxton bodies. Three were allocated to the Feathers fleet and one is seen outside the Castleton Hotel in Paignton on a tour to the West Country. Note the blinds on the cove windows to shelter travellers from the sun. The driver proudly standing in front of his coach is Major Elphee who later moved to Devon to work for Wallace Arnold there and retired in 1989. It was once common practice for drivers to have photographs like this taken as mementoes for their passengers. *M Elphee*

The Wallace Arnold office at Vaughan Road, Torquay, in the late 1950s. Tour prices range from 5s 6d (28p) for Buckfast Abbey and the Dart Valley, to 19s 6d (98p) for a full-day outing to Newquay. The full day tours all leave around 9am and return around 8.45pm, while the afternoon trips depart at 2pm, returning in time for tea at 6pm. Day tours opened up the countryside for holiday makers without cars.

Planes and boats and trains and coaches

1960s modernity at Torquay booking office. Elaborately painted boards promote excursions to Buckfast Abbey for 5s 6d (27p), Looe and Polperro for 16s 6d (82p) and Princetown and Plymouth for 13s 6d (67p). Competition in the form of a pleasure steamer lurks in the background. A Hillman Minx is prominent in the car park.

THE 1960S STARTED with a resurgence of interest in lightweight coaches. The solitary Ford operated in 1959 had impressed the company sufficiently for it to buy 10 and hire a further five which ran until 1961/62. Six Bedford SBls were also hired for various periods from a few months to two years. The Fords were bodied by Duple; the Bedfords by Plaxton.

Ford must have been well-pleased with their success in winning Wallace Arnold orders in the early 1960s. Between 1960 and 1963 a total of 47 joined the fleet compared with only 12 Bedfords. The balance swung back to Bedford from 1964 and Fords played but a small part in Wallace Arnold's operations for the remainder of the 1960s.

Leyland's new Leopard chassis was launched in 1959 and Wallace Arnold was one of the first customers, buying a single Plaxton-bodied example for evaluation. The Leopard had a larger and more powerful engine than the Tiger Cub which it ultimately replaced. A Wallace Arnold Leopard made the 4,214-mile journey from Leeds to Moscow in 1961 and featured in Leyland's advertising of the time. It was to be almost 20 years before another Wallace Arnold coach journeyed to the Soviet Union. From 1962 Leylands outnumbered AECs in each year's purchases apart from 1966.

A new double-deck bus, the first since 1954, was purchased in 1960 for the Kippax & District fleet. This was a Leyland Titan PD3 with 73-seat bodywork built by Charles H Roe. It set the standard for future double-deck purchases with a further six (of the revised PD3A model) joining the fleets of Kippax & District (three), Farsley Omnibus Co (two) and Hardwick's (one) between 1962 and 1966.

The decade had got off to a bad start with poor weather in 1960 depressing demand for leisure travel. However the market recovered in 1961 which saw a record number of bookings for the company's holiday coach tours, not only from Leeds, but also with incoming tourists arriving in London. Another record was set in 1962, but the company's directors - proudly noting that they offered holidays from Orkney to Ibiza - warned of change ahead: "Private car competition is likely to increase at a fast rate." Recognising this the Barr & Wallace Arnold Trust had already established a car sales operation - Wallace Arnold Sales & Service. Whichever way the future of leisure travel went, the group was not going to lose out.

The continental holiday programme included not only coach tours - which now embraced Norway - but also holidays by air and rail. The coach tours used local operators on the European mainland on the lower priced holidays to Belgium and Holland, and on tours to Norway. For other destinations Wallace Arnold's own coaches continued to be used throughout.

By 1961 the company was running three main British holiday programmes - Highlight holidays, Popular holidays and Feathers Cresta holidays - all now in a single comprehensive brochure, even though Feathers still had a distinctive identity with its coaches in blue and silver rather than in Wallace Arnold's ivory. Dream Holidays for the elderly (aged over 55) merited a separate brochure from 1960 and were being operated by Feathers from Bradford, Leeds, Brighouse, Halifax, Hebden Bridge, Shipley, Bingley, Stanningley Bottom, Wakefield, Castleford and Pontefract. The destinations were generally coastal resorts and departures were still outside

Small vehicles have never played more than a small part in Wallace Arnold's operations. The first, and smallest, was this 11-seat Morris J2BM which operated from 1960 to 1965 providing a feeder service to the main tour departure point in Leeds. It was Wallace Arnold's only Morris. The vehicles in the background are interesting period pieces - a modern Thames Trader pantechnicon, a Hillman Minx, a Morris Minor and a prewar Austin. *J S Cockshott*

After running one hired Thames 570E in 1959, the company purchased 10 and hired a further six in 1960. All 16 had 41-seat Duple Yeoman coachwork. Three are smartly posed at the company's stylish Scarborough garage and booking office, above which the Full Gospel of Christian Fellowship met six times a week. The BP petrol pumps are of a style now consigned to history. These attractive coaches were sold in 1965-66.

Travel on the continent
Travel on the Continent is by Wallace Arnold luxury Leyland and AEC Motor Coaches, each one costing over £5,000.
from Continental Holidays 1960 brochure

the main summer season.

By 1966 the Feathers name had been dropped from the programme (although it later reappeared) and the destinations had been extended to include key European resorts, most of which used local coaches in mainland Europe. Only a 14-day trip to the Costa Brava for 28 guineas (£29.40) used a Wallace Arnold coach throughout.

Orders for heavy-duty coaches were still being split between AEC and Leyland. The regulations limiting the length of buses and coaches were relaxed in 1961, increasing the legal maximum from 30ft to 11m (36ft 1in). Wallace Arnold was quick to take advantage of this and 18 of the 28 new coaches which joined the fleet in 1962 were to the new maximum length with 49 seats, the company's biggest coaches yet. Coaches of this size generally became the company's standard except in the lightweight day excursion fleet which continued to be made up of 41-seat Fords and Bedfords, and in Devon where road conditions dictated the use of more compact coaches for local excursions.

Both Bedford and Ford responded to the revised length legislation with 11m-long chassis. Bedford's was the revolutionary twin-steer VAL, Ford's the 676E. The VAL appeared first, and

three were hired by Wallace Arnold from Stanley Hughes for 1963-64. The VAL's three-axle layout gave a smooth ride but the brakes on its small wheels needed frequent relining and the twin-steer layout gave problems with tyre scrub. The Bedford VALs were followed by a trio of hired Ford 676Es in 1964. The VAL featured in Wallace Arnold's annual new coach intake until 1969. The 676E, and its successor the R226, were less reliable in operation and were used in smaller numbers. Both types, whether hired or purchased, had standard front-entrance coachwork, usually by Plaxton on the Bedfords and Duple on the Fords.

However the company's heavy-duty coaches, virtually all of which were purchased for a seven or eight year operating life, continued to be specified with a centre door. This practice, which had started with the introduction of underfloor-engined coaches to the fleet in 1951, came to an end in 1966-67. All of the 21 AEC Reliances delivered in 1966 had centre-entrance Plaxton bodies, as did three short Reliances delivered in 1967 for the company's Devon fleet. But the bulk of the 1967 new coach delivery, 15 Leyland Leopards, had standard front-entrance Plaxton bodies and with them the centre-entrance coach came to an end. The last of the centre-entrance coaches in the fleet was sold in 1977.

AEC supplied 24 Reliances in 1960 and all had 41-seat Plaxton bodies. The Old Mill Inn at Spinningdale offers rest and refreshments on a Scottish Highlands tour. *A D Broughall*

Bedfords had faded from Wallace Arnold's orders in the late 1950s but after buying one in 1959 the company hired six for the Wardways fleet, taken over in March 1960. These had Plaxton bodies. All were operated for only one or two seasons. The Mecca Fisheries provides sustenance on a Redcar excursion in 1960. *J S Cockshott*

A major change of image came in 1968. One of the new Leyland Leopards delivered that year was equipped as a 30-seat executive coach and was delivered from Plaxton in a new grey and white livery, instead of the familiar deep cream. From 1969 all new coaches - except those for the Devon fleet - were delivered in grey and white with a bold orange WA logo on the side. This livery was applied to existing coaches as they became due for repaint. Within a few years the entire fleet was in the new grey livery - apart from in Devon. The Devon-based operation retained the deep cream livery, but with the new WA logo.

Expansion by acquisition had continued during the 1960s, starting in March 1960 with the takeover of Wardways of Bingley. Wardways ran ten coaches, all of which were sold within weeks of the takeover. However the Wardways name was retained and the operation immediately upgraded with the delivery of six new Bedford SBIs. A small Scarborough operator, Burgess, with four coaches, was taken over in April 1961 and its ageing fleet sold. Wallace Arnold's southern operations received a boost in 1962 when it took over the tours licences of United Counties, giving the company new pick-up points in Bedford, Luton and Northampton.

Scotland was a major holiday destination and in 1962 Wallace Arnold bought the Craiglynne Hotel in Grantown-on-Spey, which was used by a number of the company's Highland tours. Its efforts to establish a customer base in Scotland had been thwarted by the Scottish Bus Group of companies who used the licensing system to protect the tour programmes run by their own subsidiaries, particularly Alexander's in Glasgow and Scottish Omnibuses in Edinburgh.

However Wallace Arnold set the cat among the pigeons in October 1963 by buying Dickson of Dundee, an established coach operator with licences for excursions and tours from Dundee, to which Wallace Arnold soon added new English holidays from Glasgow and Edinburgh, although not without a battle against stiff opposition from SBG. Dickson ran 16 coaches, eight of which were sold immediately. The others ran for varying lengths of time with two of Dickson's newest coaches surviving in Wallace Arnold ownership until 1971. The Dickson name was not retained. Wallace Arnold was anxious to imprint its own identity on the Scottish holiday coach tour business.

By 1966 it was offering three conventional coach touring holidays to English destinations, coach/air holidays to the Isle of Man, Jersey and Southern Ireland, and a Northern Ireland tour which used a Western SMT coach between Glasgow and Stranraer but the company's own coaches in Northern Ireland. A comprehensive elderly person's Dream Holidays rogramme was offered too, developing a lucrative market which the established Scottish operators had ignored.

Wallace Arnold's other Scottish involvement in the 1960s was a link with Skye Cars of Broadford whereby Wallace Arnold promoted and acted as an agent for the once-a-week summer express service between Glasgow and Portree. The journey took 10 hours and cost £4 return. In the mid-1960s Wallace Arnold took the service over from Skye Cars.

The company's southern catchment area grew in 1963 with the takeover of the goodwill

Green Alpine Valleys, Blue Lakes and Wondrous Scenery and a visit to the famous Passion Play, with reserved seats. A Panorama Scenic Holiday by Wallace Arnold Limousine Motor Coach.
from Continental Holidays 1960 brochure

The Forth Bridge, opened in 1890, provides a dramatic backdrop to a 1961 AEC Reliance on a Scottish tour. This well-appointed 41-seat coach weighed only $6^{1}/_{2}$ tons. The driver posing in Scottish headgear is Ted Harland, who was still a popular Scottish tour driver 30 years later.

garage in Donisthorpe Street until the Gelderd Road depot was completed.

In 1966 Wallace Arnold again tackled the Lancashire holiday business, this time securing licences to operate a tour programme which it was able to build upon. Pick-ups were authorised in Manchester, Liverpool and Preston. At the same time it introduced the brand name Red Carpet for its coach holidays in Britain and Ireland, using comedian Ken Dodd to help launch the new programme. The Red Carpet branding was later extended to continental air holidays.

Wallace Arnold's participation in express services increased from 1967 when it provided coaches for the South West Clipper, a marketing identity for routes from Yorkshire to the south-west of England which were largely operated by members of Associated Motorways, a loose grouping of major express coach operators. The company's involvement was primarily the provision of Friday night services from Leeds to the West Country running via Cheltenham - at that time a great express coach interchange - to Paignton, Newquay and Bournemouth. Two drivers were used, allowing for a day-time northbound return run on the Saturday. Travellers using the services would spend one or two weeks in the resorts being served.

The journey from Leeds to Cheltenham took 6 hours 15 minutes and cost 45s 6d (£2.27) return.

Gillards of Normanton was taken over in 1968. Recognising that some local goodwill was attached to the business two new coaches delivered in 1969 carried the Gillards name.

A major takeover in February 1969 saw Wallace Arnold acquire London coach operator Evan Evans. It was an apparently successful sightseeing operator, with strong business amongst incoming foreign tourists. The purchase was designed to strengthen Wallace Arnold's position in London, particularly in relation to dealing with overseas visitors. To some extent it did that, but not without difficulty. The Evan Evans fleet totalled 61 coaches, of which 23 were cramped 12-seat Commer LB minibuses. They were operated for one season; all had gone by the spring of 1970 as Wallace Arnold decided this was one sector of the tourist market which could not be developed profitably - or to the standards of comfort with which the Wallace Arnold name was associated.

of Hallen Coaches of Bristol, which brought with it licences for continental tours from the city. In 1963 Wallace Arnold won the contract from RCA to transport staff to the Fylingdales early warning station in north Yorkshire. Ten 1960 Ford 570E coaches were initially allocated to this work, later handled by heavyweight coaches which were no longer suitable for front-line excursion work. These were normally changed every two years.

The early 1960s saw dramatic growth. In 1963 the number of passengers on the company's continental air and coach holidays doubled; in 1964 the rise was 50 per cent. It also saw a surprising piece of diversification with the formation of the Northern Computer Bureau, to make computing time available to small companies. Wallace Arnold was at this time introducing computerisation to its own administration. The company was also expanding its interest in travel agencies, with a number of acquisitions, notably in Edinburgh and Leicester.

Work on a new Leeds coach depot on a 10 acre site at Gelderd Road started in 1964. It became operational in October 1966. The move was necessary because expansion of the car sales business had led the company to redevelop the Hunslet Road coach depot as a car sales and service centre. The coach fleet was temporarily housed in a former Leeds City Transport bus

In 1961 Plaxton Embassy bodywork was supplied on 18 AEC Reliances and eight of Leyland's new Leopard chassis - the Leopard was a heavier and more powerful chassis than Leyland's Tiger Cub. A Reliance waits for its passengers outside the Grand Hotel in Fort William. Note the sunvisor above the windscreen, a fitment which some might regard as optimistic on a Scottish tour. *D Akrigg/R F Mack*

The company's fleet of double-deck buses had been modernised in 1956-57 with eight rebodied Daimlers. The first new 'decker since 1954 was a Roe-bodied Leyland Titan PD3, delivered in 1960. With 73 seats it was also the company's biggest bus. It was allocated to the Kippax fleet. *A D Broughall*

Three Duple-bodied Thames Traders joined the Feathers fleet in 1961. This one is seen on a well-laden excursion in East Witton in 1964, its last season of operation. *D Akrigg*

Even the 38 full-size Evan Evans coaches were not exactly desirable vehicles. No fewer than 26 of them were modern Fords, delivered in 1968. But they had bodies by Strachans of Hamble, a company with no reputation in the manufacture of luxury coaches and whose products could not stand comparison with those of major builders Plaxton and Duple. These had to be operated for the 1969 season but 16 were withdrawn and sold as soon as the season was over and the surviving 10, which were repainted in Wallace Arnold's new grey livery, were disposed of in the spring of 1970.

The company's 1969 annual report - in what might have been a mastery of understatement - said that "the Evan Evans reorganisation and vehicle replacement proved more expensive than anticipated." Strachans-bodied Fords had little resale value.

Evan Evans had been one of the first London coach operators to tap the market for executive coach travel and operated two luxurious coaches with reclining seats, tables and well-stocked bars. Both were 11m long and one seated only 27 people in a Plaxton body, while the other carried 30 in a Duple body at a time when a maximum-capacity 11m coach had 53 seats. They were named Black Knight and Quicksilver and had liveries - black and silver respectively - to match. But even here there was a snag. Evan Evans had had their flagship coaches built on rear-engined Daimler Roadliner chassis with Cummins V6 engines. The Roadliner was disastrously unreliable. To try to improve reliability Wallace Arnold re-powered one of the coaches with a Perkins V8 engine in the summer of 1970, but Perkins power did not really solve the problems. The Cummins engine was bad; the Perkins was no better. Both coaches were sold in 1972. Five additional Roadliners which had been ordered by Evan Evans were cancelled.

The only other ex-Evan Evans coaches to survive any length of time were five Plaxton-bodied Fords (arguably the only conventional coaches in an unconventional fleet) and a small Duple-bodied Bedford VAS. All had gone by 1972. Nine new Bedford coaches were drafted in to the Evan Evans fleet in 1969, and more followed throughout the 1970s as Wallace Arnold raised standards in its London operation.

The greatest holiday organisation in Britain
Every day throughout the length and breadth of Britain and Europe, the beautiful summer ivory coloured Wallace Arnold limousine coaches can be seen driving along the picturesque holiday routes with happy people enjoying the easy relaxed way of travel. W.A. own 300 of the best limousine coaches that money can buy. Chauffeur Driven by men specially trained to take good care of you.
from 1961 Holidays in Britain and Ireland brochure

One Harrington-bodied coach operated for Wallace Arnold in the 1960s. It was an AEC Reliance with 43-seat Cavalier-style body and was on hire from Hughes for the summer of 1962. This rare view shows it parked in London's Victoria Coach Station. *D Akrigg*

The final 1960s acquisition was rather different. In December 1969 Apex Miniature Luxury Coaches of Pudsey was purchased. Apex ran two 1968 Ford Transits on feeder operations to Wallace Arnold tours. These were replaced in 1970 by a 1969 Bedford VAS transferred from the Evan Evans fleet, and a 1968 Bedford J2 from the main Wallace Arnold fleet. The Apex name survived until 1975.

All of the 1960s acquisitions were coach operators. The company was reappraising its local bus operations. The Hardwick's services at Scarborough were retained, but in the light of government plans to form passenger transport authorities in the major conurbations it was decided to give up the local operations in Leeds of Kippax & District and the Farsley Omnibus Co. The government's proposals for integrated public transport were described coldly in Wallace Arnold's 1968 annual report as "incompatible with the future growth and development of these companies".

So in March 1968 the routes operated by Kippax and Farsley were sold to Leeds City Transport. Three Alexander-bodied Leyland Panther buses on order for the Farsley fleet were cancelled. At the time of the sale Farsley operated four double-deckers and Kippax ran seven. Two of the more modern Leyland Titans were transferred to the Hardwick's fleet to replace older buses; the rest were sold. As well as having ordered Panther buses the company was actively considering buying Panther chassis for its coach fleet too. But the experience of the few coach operators running rear-engined Panthers convinced Wallace Arnold that it would be better staying with the reliable mid-engined Leopard.

Diversification - travel agencies, computers, motor dealerships - was strengthening the group but also changing the balance of its profit sources. In 1965 just over 80 per cent of its profits came from coach, bus and tour activities. By 1967 this figure was down to 53 per cent, as the group's other interests expanded.

Wallace Arnold, as befits Yorkshire's major coach operator, has played a key part in significant sporting events in the area - this is the return of the Leeds United team from the cup final in 1965. A ribbon-bedecked 1963 Leyland Leopard tours the city's streets with the team which had lost to Liverpool.

Operators acquired 1960-69		
Year	**Operator**	**No of vehicles**
1960	Wardways Ltd, Bingley	10
1961	C Burgess, Scarborough	4
1963	J Dickson Jnr, Dundee	16
1969	Evan Evans, London	61
1969	Apex, Pudsey	2

Simple design. Looking deceptively modern and very light and airy, this is a 1963 Plaxton Embassy body.

To cater for operators wanting 11m-long coaches Bedford developed the front-engined twin-steer VAL. Three were operated by Wallace Arnold in 1963-64, on hire from Hughes. They had Plaxton bodies with 52 seats - the highest capacity yet in a Wallace Arnold coach. The VAL was the only twin-steer coach chassis to reach series production in Britain. *G Stainthorpe*

Two AEC Reliances with Plaxton Panorama bodies were among the vehicles taken over from Dickson of Dundee in 1963. They were new in 1962 and ran for Wallace Arnold until 1971, latterly as part of the Hardwick's fleet in Scarborough. *D Akrigg*

In 1964 the company received 17 Leyland Leopard PSU3s with Plaxton Embassy 49-seat bodies. This one, with silver cups on the dashboard, won the Coach of the Year prize at the 1964 National Coach Rally.

Coachwork represents a cross-section of the industry. There are about 90 Plaxton bodies, slightly fewer Burlingham and examples from Duple, Roe, Leyland, Yeates and Bellhouse-Hartwell. They are uniformly smart in cream and red livery. They are free from any fitting that might be regarded as outre or extravagant for the purpose, but have the loudspeaker arrangements that are essential to the tourist and an upholstery moquette specially made for the company.
from an article in The Commercial Motor, February 5, 1960

Ford's answer to the demand for 11m-long coaches was the Thames 676E and three were taken into the Wallace Arnold fleet in 1964. All were hired from Hughes. This vehicle was allocated to the Feathers fleet and had 49-seat Plaxton bodywork. It was operated until 1966. It is loading in Leeds for an eight-day Isle of Wight tour in August 1964. *J S Cockshott*

This Leopard delivered in 1964 was an odd-man-out in the fleet in that it had Plaxton Highway bus-style bodywork. It had 51 high-backed seats, giving a higher standard of comfort than most buses, and was allocated to the Farsley fleet until 1968 when it was transferred to Hardwicks. It was withdrawn in 1972. *M Fowler*

Leyland made an unsuccessful foray into the market for lightweight coaches with the Albion Victor VT21L. Wallace Arnold tried two in 1964. Both were hired from Hughes and had stylish 41-seat Duple (Northern) Firefly bodies which were built at the erstwhile Burlingham factory in Blackpool. One operated for one season; the other for two. This one is seen parked in Leyburn Market Place. These were Wallace Arnold's first - and only - new Albions since 1930. The Victor had a vertical engine alongside the driver. *D Akrigg*

Small numbers of Bedford SB5s were purchased in the early 1960s. This one, loading at The Calls in Leeds for a coach/air holiday to Opatija in Yugoslavia was operated from 1964 to 1966. It had a Duple Bella Vega body. The destination screen, mounted vulnerably in the bumper, was a short-lived design feature. *J S Cockshott*

In 1965 Leyland supplied 18 Leopards and two Titans - the highest number of new Leylands to be taken into stock since 1947. Plaxton coachwork, still with a centre entrance, was specified for 15 of the Leopards. This one loads in Northampton bus station on an eight-day Scottish tour in 1969, after being repainted in the new two-tone grey livery adopted that year. Alongside a United Counties Bristol Lodekka is ready for an altogether more mundane trip to Cambridge. *A D Broughall*

Duple (Northern) bodied the other three 1965 Leopards which were hired from Hughes and included this 11m-long 51-seater Continental. It is seen in Edinburgh outside the Bruntsfield Hotel, a popular stopping-off point on Wallace Arnold's Scottish tours. *Gavin Booth*

Six Thames 676Es with Duple Marauder coach bodies were added to the fleet in 1965 and operated until 1967 - all were hired from Hughes. Scarborough sea front is the location of this excursion coach which is passing an Austin A40 Somerset and being followed by a rare Bristol 405 drop-head coupé. *J S Cockshott*

1966 was the last year in which AEC supplied a significant proportion of Wallace Arnold's new coaches. A total of 17 Reliances, all bodied by Plaxton, was supplied, of which five were in Feathers livery. This one required a whole Skye ferry to itself on a 1966 tour to the Scottish highlands and islands. *A J Douglas*

Perhaps the strangest coach to be operated in the 1960s was this Bedford VAL with unusual MCW Topaz II bodywork. It was hired from Hughes - and it may just be that Hughes could find no other way of getting such a strange coach off their hands. MCW, a respected bus builder, built very few coach bodies. It was operated by Wallace Arnold from 1965 to 1967 - but by 1969 was in the hands of a factory for use as staff transport. The body cost £3,600. The anodised wheel embellishers fitted to the Wallace Arnold coach were an extra-cost option at £19 15s (£19.75) for the set of six. *J S Cockshott*

The Bedford VAL continued to be favoured for excursions where its high capacity was useful. A fleet of 18 was delivered in 1966. Six went to the Kitchin fleet and one of these is seen on an excursion to the Dales, followed by a well-laden Austin 1300. *D Akrigg*

The last of the front-engined 41-seat lightweight coaches, Wallace Arnold's standard excursion vehicles of the late 1950s and early 1960s, were delivered in 1965. These included the company's last Bedford SB, a Plaxton-bodied SB5, seen with coach/air holiday passengers at Southend Airport. It was hired from Hughes and operated until 1967. Wallace Arnold had operated a total of 26 new Bedford SBs and 49 Thames 570Es - the Bedfords over a period of 15 years; the Thames over a period of seven. *T M Smith*

One of 17 Plaxton Embassy-bodied AEC Reliances delivered to Wallace Arnold in 1966 is put through its paces on the road section of the British Coach Rally. This was the last big batch of centre-entrance coaches on which the front seat passengers sat alongside the driver.

The last new double-deckers were a pair of Leyland Titan PD3As delivered in 1966. As with previous PD3s they had 73-seat Roe bodies. One was allocated to Hardwick's and the other to Farsley Omnibus. This is Pudsey bus station in February 1968. Wallace Arnold's car and truck sales activities are promoted on the side of the vehicle, standard practice for the company's Leeds area double-deck buses. An AEC Regent V of Yorkshire Woollen District stands in the background. *R Marshall*

A Plaxton-bodied Leyland Leopard passes through Strathaven in the summer of 1970 on its way to the Isle of Bute. It was one of 17 Leopards delivered in 1968 - the last year of the traditional summer ivory livery - and was one of a number of short vehicles required to meet ferry restrictions on crossings to Rothesay and Dunoon. *A J Douglas*

For 1966 Ford dropped the Thames name from its goods and passenger chassis, relaunching them simply as Fords. The Thames 676E was replaced by the Ford R226 and six Duple-bodied examples were delivered to Wallace Arnold on two-year hire from Hughes. This one was allocated to the Feathers fleet. It has Duple's new Mariner body which was in effect a face-lifted Trooper. *D Akrigg/R F Mack*

Bedford's front-engined VAM range of coach chassis was introduced in 1966 and small numbers were hired from Hughes between 1967 and 1970. The first examples had 45-seat Plaxton Panorama bodies. This is one of three in Feathers livery. The use of fixed windows and forced-air ventilation eliminated the draughts caused by sliding windows and was rapidly becoming the norm on British coaches. *D Akrigg*

Quicksilver was the pride of the Evan Evans fleet. It was a comprehensively-equipped executive coach with a bar at the front and a lounge at the rear. Its Duple Commander III body had only 30 seats. It was based on a Daimler Roadliner SRC6 chassis and was operated by Wallace Arnold, in its original silver livery, until 1972. The Houses of Parliament provide a suitably prestigious backdrop.

1968 was a year of change. Plaxton's flat-sided Embassy body was replaced by the new Panorama Elite with gently curved side windows. And Wallace Arnold's familiar summer ivory livery was replaced by a new two-tone grey relieved by a large orange WA logo and white fleetnames. The result was striking - it was the work of the Ogle design consultancy - and one of the first coaches to wear it was this Bedford VAL which was an exhibit on Plaxton's stand at the 1968 Commercial Motor Show at Earls Court. It was one of four VALs, Wallace Arnold's last, which entered service in 1969. *R H G Simpson*

The majority of Evan Evans' full-sized coaches were Fords with unusual Strachans bodies which were neither particularly stylish nor particularly durable. There were 26 of these strange machines, ten of which were transferred to Yorkshire and survived with Wallace Arnold for the duration of the 1970 season and were repainted in fleet livery. *D Akrigg*

1969 was one of Leyland's best years with Wallace Arnold. A fleet of 35 Plaxton-bodied Leopards was delivered, a figure which was only equalled once more (in 1978) and exceeded only once, in 1981. Most were 49-seaters, including this vehicle seen in London's Piccadilly after being transferred to the Evan Evans fleet in 1971. *D Akrigg*

Expansion in Europe

IN 1970 THE Leyland Leopard was effectively Wallace Arnold's standard coach and Plaxton was the company's main body supplier - which it had been since the late 1950s. The last small batches of AECs entered service in 1971 and 1972. There was still a steady flow of Bedfords (which became a trickle after 1975) and a very small number of Fords joining the fleet. But between 1970 and 1979 Leyland supplied 289 Leopards out of a total of 385 coaches delivered in the decade.

Plaxton's sales successes were equally remarkable with the supply of 251 coach bodies against Duple's 134, although this figure masks Duple's successes in 1976 (when it supplied all the company's bodywork) and in 1977/78 when it supplied many more than Plaxton. Duple's success was short-lived. In 1979 Wallace Arnold's body order was divided equally between Duple and Plaxton. No further Duple bodies were purchased until 1986/7 and then only in small numbers.

A new depot for the Devon fleet was opened in Barton Hill, Torquay, in June 1970.

Mercedes-Benz, who had periodically tried to interest British operators in its integral coaches, loaned a new O.302 demonstrator to Wallace Arnold in 1971. The coach was purchased by the company but it was considerably more expensive to buy and to operate than the comparatively simple Leyland Leopards and no more Mercedes coaches were tried until the German manufacturer's next major offensive on the UK coach market in 1990. The O.302 was the first air-suspended coach owned by Wallace Arnold. Air suspension was not to become widely-accepted in Britain until the early 1980s.

The only Bristols to be owned by Wallace Arnold were purchased in 1975 for its Devon operations. Six Leyland-engined LH6Ls with 45-seat 10m-long Plaxton bodies were used on excursions in the south west. The LH, in its 11m long LHL variant, was also considered for the Evan Evans operation. It offered a combination of durability and a comparatively low initial purchase price which seemed appealing for London-based operations. But in the end Evan Evans received standard Leylands, Fords and Bedfords.

After a bad start, the Evan Evans operation moved into profit in 1971, although by the middle of the decade the directors' verdict on Evan Evans' profits was that they were "not yet satisfactory". The company's best year was 1977, when the Queen's Silver Jubilee gave a boost to the whole London tourist trade. By the end of the decade it was in the red again. Part of the problem was that many of the seats on Evan Evans tours were sold by hotel porters which made it difficult to gauge passenger numbers in advance and to plan operations accordingly. An enterprising innovation by Evan Evans in 1975 was a London sightseeing tour which included a trip on the

Wallace Arnold and its drivers have been frequent entrants in the British Coach Rally. Going through its paces on Brighton's Madeira Drive in 1971 is a new Leyland Leopard, one of 29 delivered that year. It has 53-seat Plaxton Panorama Elite coachwork. *G R Mills*

Thames in a Hydrofoil from the Tower of London to Greenwich and back. To service the southern activities of the main Wallace Arnold fleet a new depot was opened in Croydon.

The profitable day excursion business in Leeds and Bradford had been in steady decline since the boom days of the 1950s. Increased car ownership was reducing demand for day trips by coach, although until the mid-1970s Wallace Arnold was often sending as many as 10 coaches to Blackpool and Scarborough and a further 10 to Bridlington on a good bank holiday.

In contrast with the declining day excursion business, the decade started with a rapid expansion in continental holidays -in 1971 Wallace Arnold's continental tour programme offered 36,000 seats. This was increased to 42,000 for 1972, a rise of 33 per cent. Coach/air holidays were being operated using Swissair DC9s from Manchester, British Caledonian BAC1-11s from Gatwick and Court Line BAC1-11s from Luton. The Red Carpet brand name on

The long and the short. Nearest the camera is one of three 1972 Bedford VAS5s with 29-seat Plaxton body. Alongside stands a 57-seat Plaxton-bodied AEC Reliance, one of two delivered in 1971 - the company's first 12m-long coaches and the biggest yet operated. A total of eight AEC Reliances was delivered in 1971, followed by one in 1972 which was to be the company's last AEC. The first new AEC had been purchased in 1933 and AEC had been a major supplier to Wallace Arnold in the 1950s. The last of the AECs was sold in 1975. *A N Mountjoy*

Mercedes Benz was looking for prestigious British operators to run its expensive O.302 integral coaches. This demonstrator was supplied to Wallace Arnold, painted in the company's livery, in the spring of 1971 and was purchased a few months later. It was the company's first new rear-engined coach - and, other than the ex-Evan Evans Roadliners, the only one to be operated until 1982. It is seen at the 1971 British Coach Rally in Brighton. *G R Mills*

continental air holidays was superseded by WallaceAir in 1972. At the same time coach connections from Bradford, Leeds, Leicester, Wakefield and Sheffield to Luton and Gatwick airports were promoted under the Aerolink name. Scottish holidaymakers could fly from Glasgow.

The Devon company ran holiday coach tours as well as local excursions for incoming visitors and its holiday programme received a boost in 1973 with the granting of licences to pick up passengers at Taunton, Bridgwater and Bristol. In the north new pick-ups were introduced on UK tours at Sheffield, Rotherham, Barnsley and Doncaster. And despite opposition in the West Midlands the company won licences to run from Birmingham, Wolverhampton and Coventry - initially only for one year, although this was subsequently extended.

The opening of the M62 motorway across the Pennines saw Wallace Arnold apply for licences to run feeder services from Lancashire to connect with its main Yorkshire-based tour programme. This move attracted objections from no fewer than 21 other operators and after lengthy traffic court hearings the application was rejected by the traffic commissioners - only to be granted when the company lodged an appeal with the Environment Secretary who had the ultimate say in licensing disputes.

One battle which the company did not win was based on plans announced in 1973 for Evan Evans to run cheap coach services for students. These would have linked London with 12 university destinations - Leicester, Loughborough, Nottingham, Aston, Birmingham, Sheffield, Leeds, Bradford, Salford, Manchester, Bath and Bristol. Not surprisingly the licence applications attracted opposition from 12 existing express coach operators and from British Rail.

The aftermath of the industrial unrest which afflicted Britain in the early 1970s saw Wallace Arnold cut its continental touring programme in the middle of the decade: the market for continental holidays dropped by 50 per cent between 1973 and 1974 and saw some major operators - notably Court Line - in trouble. Wallace Arnold had been using Court Line for coach/air holidays through Luton Airport but was able to record that not one single holiday was lost as a result of the Court Line collapse.

Express Rail holidays to Spain and Italy, with prices from £59 for 10 days from London, were launched in 1975. These used scheduled rail services. At the same time Wallace Arnold was seeking to develop another new market. Air fares in Europe were high, demand for cross-European travel was growing. So the company sought to launch scheduled services from London to Rome, Barcelona, Marseilles, Munich, Basle and Milan, taking advantage of Britain's membership of the EEC and hoping to create new travel markets amongst young and elderly persons.

Agreement was reached in 1975 with operators in Paris and Florence for a jointly-operated express service linking London, Paris, Lyon, Turin, Genoa, Florence and Rome. The launch of this cross-European service was hindered by European Community red tape, but finally got under way in April 1977, running once a week in the summer. A standard 49-seat Duple-bodied Leyland Leopard - which cost around £25,000 - was allocated to the operation. The end-to-end journey time was 37 hours with a return fare of £63.

This neat coach was one of only two Bedford J2s to be operated by Wallace Arnold. It was purchased from a dealer's stock in 1971 and allocated to the Devon fleet. The 20-seat body was by Plaxton. After running for a short while with its original diesel engine it was replaced with a petrol unit in the interests of smooth running and passenger comfort. It was operated until 1976. Note the Wallace Arnold coach stop sign. *D Akrigg*

In 1971 Wallace Arnold bought four 1968 rear-engined AEC Swifts from Sheffield City Transport. These had 47-seat two-door Park Royal bodies and replaced double-deckers on Hardwick's services. They were withdrawn in 1974 and replaced by Leyland Leopard coaches with bus seats. *G R Mills*

There were also plans to run to Istanbul and Vienna and the company was weighing up the alternative types of coach which might be appropriate for arduous European services. Its main supplier, Leyland, was being considered alongside Setra and Mercedes-Benz of Germany, DAF of Holland, and Leyland-DAB of Denmark as possible sources of left-hand-drive coaches if services developed.

A new subsidiary, Euroways Express Coaches, was formed in 1977 with an eye to developing this market in which Wallace Arnold's involvement reached a peak in 1979 when its new vehicle purchases included some 12m-long Plaxton-bodied Volvo B58s with 51 reclining seats. These were used on the Euroways services from London to Rome, Barcelona and Paris. Subsequently the company usually subcontracted its European express service commitments to other operators.

The company had started making limited use of 12m-long coaches in 1971. The length limit had been raised from 11m to 12m in 1969, but most coach operators chose to continue with 11m-long coaches which offered a balance between high carrying capacity and manoeuvrability - important on tours to out-of-the-way places. Three 12m-long Reliances joined the fleet in 1971-72, followed by two Leopards for the Devon operation in 1974. These had 57 seats instead of the 53 in the company's standard 11m-long coaches. A further two were allocated to the Leeds fleet in 1975. Maximum length coaches formed a small minority of new purchases for the remainder of the decade.

There were signs that tour licensing was being liberalised - a move welcomed by Wallace Arnold. As early as 1974 the company was calling for freedom in the operation of express services - something that would not come about until October 1980. Plans were actually developed at this time to introduce Wallace Arnold's own-brand up-market express coach services, to be called Motor Ways. These would have used 12m-long coaches with reclining seats and toilets. In the end the company decided that the returns which Motor Ways offered were not worth the cost and effort of a long struggle in the traffic courts to win licences.

Mercedes' sortie into the UK coach market in the early 1970s was unsuccessful, but other continental European manufacturers were seeking to develop coach sales in the UK.

Foremost amongst these was Volvo, whose mid-engined B58 chassis was a direct and more powerful competitor for Leyland's established Leopard. The Leopard used Leyland's 175bhp 680 engine where the B58 had a 230bhp turbocharged Volvo THD100D engine. Wallace Arnold first looked at Volvo in 1973, but it was not until 1977 that the decision was made to try the B58 alongside the Leyland Leopard. Six B58s were delivered in 1978. Four were operated from Leeds and two went to the Evan Evans fleet. They had Plaxton bodies, although from 1976 Duple had temporarily usurped Plaxton as the company's major body supplier. The Leeds-based Volvos had Telma retarders and semi-automatic gearboxes.

One season's experience was enough to confirm that the Volvo did have something to offer in terms of performance and reliability and to Leyland's disappointment Wallace Arnold's 1979 order was divided - 20 Leyland Leopards were to be delivered, along with 16 Volvo B58s. Little did Leyland realise that this was the beginning of the end. Its new Leopard replacement chassis, the Tiger, was in an advanced stage of development - but was going to appear too late to win Wallace Arnold's business in the 1980s.

Only one operator was taken over by Wallace Arnold in the 1970s - the Embankment Motor Co of Plymouth. Embankment was

The two-tone grey livery was not applied to the Devon fleet which retained the traditional ivory. Four of 1973's delivery of 27 Plaxton-bodied Leyland Leopards were allocated to Devon. This one illustrates the ever-growing WA logo used from 1975. *G H Truran*

Six of the 27 Leyland Leopards delivered in 1973 were allocated to Hardwick's for use initially as coaches and latterly as buses. After two seasons on coaching duties they were fitted with bus seats and the displaced coach seats were transferred to new coaches being delivered in 1975. By 1985, when this one was photographed, they were the oldest vehicles in the fleet and were operating in an orange, brown and white livery used only for Hardwick's buses.
M Fowler

purchased in May 1974 and operated a fleet of 25 modern Bedford coaches. The company operated briefly as a separate unit with the Embankment fleetname, but was integrated with the main Devon business during 1976. Its coaches were withdrawn over a four year period.

In Scotland there were still skirmishes between Wallace Arnold and the Scottish Bus Group over coach holidays. In 1975 SBG blocked Wallace Arnold's plans to expand its operations from Glasgow - but did manage to reach agreement which allowed some limited improvements to the company's Edinburgh-based programme.

There was considerable tidying up of the company's acquired subsidiaries from 1975, with a long list of inactive subsidiaries being wound up - on the coach side of the business these were Feather Bros (Tours) Ltd, Hudson's Coaches (Leeds) Ltd, J W Kitchin & Sons Ltd, Wardways Ltd, Sunbeam Garages (Torquay) Ltd, The Tidebank Co Ltd, Lismore Coaches Ltd, Charing Cross Tourist Agency Ltd, American Sightseeing Tours Ltd, Cream Cars (Torquay) Ltd and Waverley Motor Coach Tours Ltd. This tidying operation left extant six coach subsidiaries - Wallace Arnold Tours, Hardwick's Services, Evan Evans Tours, Woburn Garages (London), Wallace Arnold Tours (Devon) and Embankment Motor Co (Plymouth).

On the bus front double-deck operation came to an end when Hardwick's three Leyland Titans were withdrawn in 1971. Their replacements were four second-hand AEC Swifts which were purchased from Sheffield Transport. The Swifts had dual-door Park Royal bodies and were designed for one-man-operation. Their arrival brought to an end the use of conductors on Hardwick's services. The Swifts were not a success. The rear-engined layout offered a low floor with easy entry and exit, but it also created problems with mechanical reliability. The Swifts were only operated for three years and were replaced by Leyland Leopard coaches which were fitted with bus seats for use on Hardwick's Scarborough local services.

The group's profits exceeded £1 million for

the first time in 1976. Following the success of the London to Rome service, Wallace Arnold set its sights on a prize new destination - Moscow, which in the 1970s was still firmly behind the Iron Curtain. The forthcoming Moscow Olympics were one attraction when the service was being planned. During 1977 negotiations were concluded with Sovtransavto for a joint service to start in 1979. A trial run in 1978 gave Moscow its second taste of a Wallace Arnold coach, this time a Plaxton-bodied Volvo.

Agreement was also reached with state-owned National Travel on the operation of routes between Britain and France, Spain, Italy, Denmark and Greece, with the hope of implementing some sort of network in 1978 or 1979. Wallace Arnold anticipated the development of a European equivalent of the American Greyhound network.

In London Evan Evans was developing contract work with coaches in special liveries. Significant among these was the Hoverlloyd contract, to carry passengers from London to Ramsgate Hoverport at Pegwell Bay. This was won from National Bus Company subsidiary East Kent. Two 1976 Leopards received Hoverlloyd livery for the start of the service in October 1977 and were followed by two new Leopards in this livery in 1978. Other contract liveries included Swiss holiday companies Vingresor and London Air Tours of Geneva.

The Dream Holidays for the Elderly programme was becoming increasingly important as the decade progressed and by 1979 had been rebranded as Supersaver Holidays for the Older Holidaymaker. In the same year the Waverley rail-link programme was introduced, offering English holidaymakers fast first class rail travel to Carlisle or Glasgow to join a coach for a Scottish holiday. Waverley was more than just a coach holiday package; also on offer were centred holidays by rail and self-drive holidays using Swan National cars. By the end of the decade Wallace Arnold was running over 300 coaches which were carrying 2.5 million people and covering 10 million miles a year.

Operators acquired 1970-79		
Year	**Operator**	**No of vehicles**
1974	Embankment Motor Co Ltd, Plymouth	25

In 1974 Wallace Arnold started a new sequence of registration numbers beginning at 1, with this Leopard TUB1M. From then until 1983 every effort was made to book sequential registrations and the practice ceased with Setra FUA406Y. TUB1M is seen in Victoria Coach Station, London, on a Spanish tour. *D Akrigg*

Contracts for tour operators led to a number of Evan Evans coaches receiving special liveries in the late 1970s. This is a 1974 Leyland Leopard decorated with Shakespearean scenes to promote trips to Shakespeare's Tavern, where visitors were promised a Royal Feast. *G R Mills*

Big Bedford coaches made a brief reappearance in the fleet in the mid-1970s with the mid-engined YRQ and YRT chassis. Between 1973 and 1975 a total of 31 was hired or purchased. Four of the 1974 YRTs had 53-seat Duple Dominant bodywork - the first Dominants in the fleet. This one is seen in Moffat on a Scottish tour. *G Coxon*

The only Bristols operated by Wallace Arnold were six LH6Ls with 45-seat Plaxton bodies. They were bought in 1975 and all six were delivered in ivory with three being allocated to the Devon fleet and three to Embankment in Plymouth which was absorbed into the main Devon operation two years later. The roof-mounted destination box was necessary because the LH chassis had a front-mounted radiator which precluded the inclusion of a destination display below the windscreen. *D Akrigg*

The Embankment Motor Company fleet, operating from Plymouth, was made up entirely of Bedfords, including ten YRQs. It was taken over by Wallace Arnold in 1974. This YRQ with Duple Viceroy bodywork was retained until 1975. *D Akrigg*

Bottom left: Two 1970 Bedford SB5s acquired from Embankment were among the more unusual coaches to receive Wallace Arnold livery in the 1970s. They had special narrow Duple Vega 31 bodies.

Below: The Ford Transit featured briefly in the company's minibus fleet; nine were purchased between 1970 and 1974. This is one of the last with a 12-seat Deansgate conversion which included a roof rack for passengers' luggage. *D Akrigg*

The Embankment fleet at Plymouth was managed as part of the Devon operation and used the same livery but with Embankment fleetnames. Four short-wheelbase PSU4 Leopards with narrow (7ft 8½in) Duple Dominant bodies were delivered to Embankment in 1976. This was a period of brief resurgence for Duple in the Wallace Arnold fleet. All of the 1976 intake of new coaches had Duple bodies and between 1976 and 1979 the company supplied 115 bodies - which was as many as they had supplied in the previous 20 years. *G H Truran*

Deliveries of small Bedford VAS5s continued throughout the 1970s. Two Plaxton-bodied examples were delivered to the Devon fleet in 1975. This one is seen at Slapton Sands. *G H Truran*

Below: The final Y-series Bedfords were nine hired from Hughes in 1975 and operated until 1977. Five of these were in non-standard liveries including this Plaxton-bodied YRT seen in central Bradford. It was red and grey, coincidentally the colours once used by Kitchen. *D Akrigg*

Short wheelbase Leopards with standard 2.5m (8ft 2½in) wide bodies were delivered to the Leeds-based fleet in 1976, primarily for use on tours to the Scottish Islands. One boards a ferry on the west coast. *R L Grieves*

In 1977 a fleet of 29 Leyland Leopards with Duple Dominant bodies was delivered. One was entered in the British Coach Rally and is seen here in the Sussex countryside on the road section of the driving tests.

Winning the Hoverlloyd contract was quite a feather in Evan Evans' cap. The contract required coaches to take passengers from London to the hovercraft terminal at Ramsgate, from whence they sailed (or flew?) to Calais. Two 1976 Leopards were repainted in Hoverlloyd livery in 1977. *G H Truran*

1979 was the last year in which Duple received a large order from Wallace Arnold, supplying 17 Dominant bodies on Leyland and Volvo chassis. A Leyland Leopard swings into the independent coach terminal in Glasgow. Three more Wallace Arnold coaches are in the coach park behind. *A J Douglas*

In 1978 Wallace Arnold took delivery of a record 35 new Leylands, all Duple-bodied Leopards. Eight were allocated to Devon, including this coach seen heading towards Edinburgh after crossing the Forth Road Bridge. *John Burnett*

The company's first Volvos were delivered in 1978 with the arrival of six Plaxton-bodied B58s. Few people at Leyland - or at Volvo - could have appreciated the significance of this small order on Wallace Arnold's future coach buying policy. Two of the new Volvos were 11m-long models with 46 reclining seats for use on the Euroways London to Barcelona service. *G H Truran*

The Leyland Leopard was nearing the end of its long production life by 1979. Eight of the 20 delivered to Wallace Arnold that year were allocated to the Evan Evans fleet. This 53-seater is seen in Scarborough prior to delivery from Plaxton. The two-tone grey livery was revised for 1979 with fashionable upswept stripes in place of the previous dark grey waistband. The Plaxton body is of the new Supreme model, which was in effect a facelifted Panorama Elite. *G H Truran*

Top quality touring

EXPRESS COACH SERVICES in Britain were freed from licensing controls in October 1980. Wallace Arnold joined a number of other leading British coach operators in the British Coachways consortium, launched to break the National Express near-monopoly of intercity coaching. Unlike some British Coachways members, Wallace Arnold was careful not to underestimate National Express's experience and it watched the fledgling British Coachways operation carefully.

Three coaches were repainted in the consortium's red and blue striped livery and performed on services from Yorkshire to London and the West Country. Three of 1981's new Leopard coaches were delivered in British Coachways colours. But National Express responded vigorously, as did British Rail (with the aid of government funding) and after 12 months Wallace Arnold withdrew from British Coachways. The consortium's other members soon did likewise.

With hindsight it is easy to say that British Coachways was doomed from the start. It had too many members, many of whom were competitors united in an uneasy alliance and most of whom wanted the maximum return for the minimum risk. It was slow to react to National Express, and its terminal arrangements, particularly in London, were unsatisfactory.

However the experience gained with British Coachways led Wallace Arnold to launch its own Pullman Express service from Leeds to London at the end of 1981. This operated from the Royal National Hotel in Bloomsbury, already used for some Evan Evans excursion operations and a considerably more salubrious location than the King's Cross terminal yard of British Coachways. The service was operated by Leyland Leopards with toilets. The coaches were subsequently equipped with video systems and hostess call buttons. The Leopards were replaced in 1982 by three Bova integrals. From July that year the service was integrated with the National Express Rapide network and the Bovas were repainted in National Express white livery. Wallace Arnold withdrew from the service at the start of 1985.

For 1980 we will have over fifty brand new coaches, and most of these superb new vehicles will supplement our British tour fleet of modern, fully-equipped coaches. We enjoy a cherished reputation for impeccably maintained coaches, which is made possible by our sophisticated and comprehensively equipped central workshops, which operate round the clock, day and night.
from 1980 British holidays brochure

In 1980 Wallace Arnold took delivery of 20 Volvo B58s, all with Plaxton Supreme bodies. This one is seen in November 1980, shortly after the launch of the British Coachways express service network and is carrying a British Coachways Cityliner bill in the windscreen. The location is the rather basic London terminal of British Coachways at King's Cross. *M R Keeley*

Three of 1981's Leyland Leopards were delivered in British Coachways red, white and blue livery. This 12m PSU5 had 51-seat Plaxton bodywork and is seen at King's Cross in July 1981. *S J Butler*

The European express network flourished despite bureaucratic controls, with services to Italy, Spain, France and Switzerland. Euroways fleetnames were carried by three new Volvos delivered to the Evan Evans fleet in 1982 and one for the Devon operation in 1983. By 1984 the method of contracting vehicles for Euroways services was altered. A new company Euroways (Eurolines) was formed in 1985 and was in profit in 1986 with services to Paris, Amsterdam and Alicante. In 1989 Wallace Arnold decided to give up its European interests and sold its Euroways operations to National Express.

A new series of holidays was launched in 1980 - Coach & Cruise. For these Wallace Arnold had linked up with P&O Cruises to provide European holidays which combined coach travel with cruising on the P&O's Canberra and Oriana liners. Prices started at £364 for 12 days using the coach between Britain and Nice and returning by sea - or vice versa. Another novel holiday programme, In-Tent, was launched by the group in 1980 to provide camping holidays abroad for motoring families. It was sold in 1984. Also sold in 1984 was the group's pioneering computer services division.

Expansion continued in car dealerships and with the acquisition of a 60 per cent stake in the Regency Carriage Co, a London chauffeur-driven car hire business. This, however, was found to be a business which required extensive (and expensive) supervision and the stake was sold in 1986.

The market for holiday coach tours was generally healthy - but was becoming more competitive. Lancashire-based Smiths-Happiways-Shearings was expanding. National Holidays, consolidating the various National Bus Company operations, was trying to regain its dominant position in the 1980s and it expanded at Wallace Arnold's expense. A clever - and possibly unique - marketing ploy in the coach holiday business was a competition for the 1983 season. To encourage early

Second-hand coaches have never featured prominently in Wallace Arnold's operations, except during World War II when new vehicles were virtually unobtainable, or when they have been acquired with businesses which have been taken over. Among the few modern second-hand vehicles to have been operated were four Leyland Leopards purchased in 1980. The Leopards were all between one and two years old and ran for the Devon fleet until the end of the 1983 summer season. This 1978 Leopard PSU5 with Plaxton body was originally operated by Smith of Wilmcote. It is seen on Dartmoor in April 1982.
J Marsh

Little interest had been shown in lightweight Ford chassis during the 1970s - only 11 were taken into stock between 1970 and 1979. But a change of policy saw Ford given one last chance, with orders for 15 in 1980 and 1981. These were used to provide higher standards in the excursion and private hire fleet, operating on duties which had been covered in the 1970s by down-grading former front-line coaches. All of the Fords were R1114s with 53-seat Plaxton bodies. One of the 1981 batch approaches Bridlington in 1983. The last of the Fords was sold in 1985.
G B Wise

bookings, passengers who booked before 31 January had the opportunity to win a Volkswagen Polo. The competition was apt: contestants had to calculate the annual total mileage in the UK and Europe in 1982 of Wallace Arnold's 141 coaches.

Recognising the growing concern over the effects of smoking on health, the first no-smoking tours to be offered by Wallace Arnold were introduced in 1980. From 1983 on all tours smokers were allocated seats on the offside of the coach; non-smokers were offered seats on the nearside. This was later revised and non-smokers were given seats at the front of the coach while customers who wanted to smoke were seated at the rear. From 1991 a no-smoking policy was applied to all of the company's tours.

A new Evan Evans depot was opened in London's York Way in 1981 with room for up to 54 coaches - but it was to be short-lived. In 1983 the company admitted defeat with Evan Evans. It was sold to Insight for £40,000 in February, bringing to an end 14 years of generally troublesome operation which had started with the acquisition of a less than ideal fleet and which had contributed little to the group's profitability. The deal with Insight did not include any vehicles or property. The difficulty in recruiting and retaining skilled maintenance staff had exacerbated Evan Evans' problems and at one time as much as 20 per cent of the London-based fleet was out of service awaiting remedial work.

Having successfully identified a market amongst elderly people, Wallace Arnold aimed at the youth market with its Go Bananas holidays, introduced in 1983. Seven destinations in southern Europe were served and the brash brochure extolled the attractions of drinks, discos and even a nudist beach. Free Go Bananas T-shirts were on offer for May holidaymakers. A new Bova coach wore a yellow Go Bananas livery.

Rationalisation of the company's Yorkshire operations and a reduction in the fleet saw the closure of the depots at Castleford, Royston, Pudsey and Bradford in the early 1980s. All of the Yorkshire-based fleet was now centred on Gelderd Road. Having dual-sourced from Leyland and Volvo in 1979, the company had been favourably impressed by Volvo, apart from some gearbox troubles which helped Leyland get its last large order in 1981 when Volvo got no business at all from Wallace Arnold. However this was just a temporary difficulty.

When Leyland's new Tiger was launched in 1980, Wallace Arnold had ordered three - which thanks to confusion between Leyland and Plaxton were not built to the required specification. They were delivered late in 1981 and were to be the fleet's last new Leylands, bringing to an end an association started in 1925. New coaches in the early 1980s were Volvo's air-suspended B10M, as the successor to the B58, with a small batch of German Setra integrals, and a fleet of Dutch-built Bova integrals. The Setras, of which there were six delivered in 1982-83, were powered by Mercedes-Benz engines. The Bovas used DAF engines and the first were ordered to satisfy the needs of one tour operator, Seasons Holidays, who wanted continental-style coaches for their 1982 tours. Ultimately Wallace Arnold owned

1981 was Leyland's best year ever at Wallace Arnold. It was also its last. A total of 35 Plaxton-bodied Leopards was delivered to a variety of specifications. This is an 11m-long PSU3 with 46-seat bodywork which was allocated to Devon. It is seen unloading in Dartmouth in 1986. *G B Wise*

29 Bovas, all delivered in 1982-83.

Faced with an ever increasing choice of chassis the company weighed up the main options open to it. For 1984 it saw the choice lying between the proven Volvo/Plaxton combination, at an anticipated cost of around £62,500; the Bova Europa at £61,850; the new Bova Futura at £65,112 (3.2m high) or £68,600 (3.5m high); the combination of DAF SB with semi-integral Plaxton bodywork, expected to cost around £58,850; the Setra, at an expensive £82,000, or Leyland's new Royal Tiger Doyen integral -which was then being built at the Charles H Roe factory in Leeds - at £70,000.

A programme for discussion could have led to Wallace Arnold purchasing 16 Volvo/Plaxton, five Bova Europa, four Bova Futura, six DAF/Plaxton, two Setra and two Royal Tiger Doyens. This plan was discarded when a new management team took over and the fleet continued to standardise on the model it knew best: the Plaxton-bodied Volvo.

Subcontracting to operators who would run high-quality coaches in Wallace Arnold's livery was a feature from the mid-1980s. To the casual observer the vehicles were indistinguishable from Wallace Arnold's own. Operators who supplied coaches included Park's of Hamilton, East Yorkshire and Southdown Motor Services. The most unusual vehicle to be operated in Wallace Arnold livery was the first DAF SBR3000 three-axle double-deck coach in Britain, which was delivered to Park's in 1987. It had a 74-seat Plaxton body.

The RCA contract for Fylingdales ended in January 1985. Its final allocation comprised nine Fords. The company's Croydon depot was closed in 1985 and servicing in the south was put in the hands of London Buses at its Norwood garage.

The structure of the coach market was changing and the new management team which took over at Wallace Arnold in 1985 devised a new strategy to cope with this. Its aim was summed up in the 1987 annual report: "Our strategy is to offer good quality, value for money services - mainly to elderly people; to operate the most modern fleet of coaches in the country and to give travel agents a highly efficient booking service." This strategy was quickly implemented with promotions aimed at the over 55s; with a three-year vehicle replacement cycle; and with updating of the computer links between the company's central booking office and its 7,000-plus agents throughout the country. The reservations system had been fully computerised since 1982, but from 1985 a new on-line system gave agents direct access. The whole system was further updated at a cost of £750,000 in 1989.

An attempt was made in 1986 to resurrect coastal express services on summer Saturdays, working jointly with Yorkshire Rider, but a reappraisal of the company's operations led it to the conclusion that it was essentially a holiday tour company running coaches - and that express services had no part to play in its future business. The only adjuncts to its core operations were private hires and excursions, which could be built in around the main business.

Dictionary definition
Go Bananas. Out of this world continental holidays at down to earth prices. Exclusively for the 18-28 age group with the accent most definitely on fun. A subsidiary of the extremely conventional - day trips to Blackpool - but ever so reliable Wallace Arnold Group.
from 1983 Go Bananas brochure

By 1986 the Leopards operating on Harwick's services were over 13 years old and it was decided to upgrade the fleet prior to local bus service deregulation in October of that year. This 1981 Leopard was converted from a 49-seat coach to a 53-seat bus with power-operated doors. Photographed shortly after deregulation it carries publicity on the windows listing the principal places served between Scarborough and Ebberston and advertising that the service runs seven days a week. *R Marshall*

The privatisation of the National Bus
Company started in 1986 and the first company
to be advertised for sale was National Holidays,
one of Wallace Arnold's main rivals in the
coach holiday business. A bid was made for
National Holidays - but was beaten by a higher
bid from the Lancashire-based Smiths-Shearings
organisation.

The Hardwick's local bus operation in
Scarborough was still running, with its main
services extended through the town centre to the
company's depot, following the closure of the
East Yorkshire bus station in 1982. With local
bus service deregulation in 1986 the Hardwick's
operation was extended to Pickering and
Helmsley in the evenings and at weekends,
when the company submitted a zero tender to
run the service for North Yorkshire County
Council. In 1987 double-deck operation was re-
introduced with the purchase of two ex-Greater
Manchester Transport Leyland Atlanteans which
were converted to open top by Plaxton and used
on a new sea front service. Two ex-GMT
Leyland Nationals were also added to the fleet.

After 12 months of deregulated bus
operation Wallace Arnold again decided it
should stick with its core business and it sold its
Scarborough operations - both Hardwick's and
the excursion business - to East Yorkshire Motor
Services. EYMS acquired some of the vehicles;
the newest coaches were retained by Wallace
Arnold and returned to Leeds. The pattern of
holidaymaking in Scarborough was changing
and the excursion market - which was at one
time hotly contested by Wallace Arnold and
United Automobile Services - had shrunk
dramatically.

The gradual decline of the Glasgow-based
Cotter group saw Wallace Arnold expand in the
spring of 1987 by taking over the operations of
Cotter-owned Bee Line Tours of
Middlesborough and Florence & Grange of
Morecambe. No vehicles were acquired. The
Bee Line name was used for certain holidays
until 1989. The Florence & Grange tour
programme was quickly wound down.

In October 1987 the Cotter group closed
down and Wallace Arnold took over the
company's tour business. An extra 12 coaches
were ordered for 1988 in white and orange
Cotter's livery (but applied in Wallace Arnold
house style) and were used on Scottish-based
tours. By 1990 the Scottish programme of
Wallace Arnold had been merged with that of
Cotter, although tours were still marketed under
the Cotter name, advertised as incorporating
Watson's of Dundee.

Growth came in 1988 with the takeover of
the International Leisure Group's four main
coach holiday programmes - Global Overland,
Continental Coach, Superdeals and Golden
Circle. Wallace Arnold retained the rights to the
Overland name, but had the use of the Global
name for two years only. A "Superdeal from
Overland" programme was developed using
subcontracted coaches. The continuing
improvements in the company's performance
earned it the "Top Coach Holiday Operator of
1988" award after a poll by the magazine *Travel
Trade Gazette* of over 6,500 travel agents. It
won the same award in 1989. By 1990 Wallace
Arnold was carrying around 250,000 people a
year making it the second-largest coach tour
operator in Britain.

Leyland's new air-suspended Tiger was developed to
replace the Leopard and beat the Volvo. Wallace
Arnold took three in 1981, but despite Leyland's
hopes, they were to be Wallace Arnold's last Leyland
chassis, bringing to an end a tie which stretched back
almost 60 years to 1925 and during which time over
600 new Leylands had passed through Wallace
Arnold's fleet. A Plaxton-bodied Tiger stands
alongside a 1983 Setra integral. *M Fowler*

For 1982 Wallace Arnold ordered rear-engined integral coaches from two continental European manufactures. The first to arrive, in March, came from Bova who supplied 15 of their Europa model. These had a non-standard livery layout with an orange relief band ahead of the WA logo and a brown band to the rear. The fleetname was also in a non-standard style: the Arnold name started with a rounded capital A instead of the normal pointed type. The Bovas had 8.2-litre turbocharged DAF engines. This one is seen on the Thames embankment at Pimlico in the company of a 1981 Leyland Leopard. *M Fowler*

Two of the 1982 Bovas were repainted in white National Express Rapide livery in 1983 for use on services from Yorkshire to London which had previously been run by Wallace Arnold under the Pullman Express title. These coaches were 47 seaters with a toilet compartment. Wallace Arnold operated on the London service until 1985. *Stewart J Brown*

Interest in Bedfords, once a major supplier to Wallace Arnold, had diminished in the 1970s and finally came to an end in 1983. The last Bedfords were a pair of short YMQ-S models with 31-seat Plaxton bodies for operation in Devon. The first Bedford to operate for Wallace Arnold joined the fleet in 1938; over 200 were operated in the following 45 years. *G R Mills*

In 1983 the company bought 17 Volvos, now of the improved B10M model with air suspension. These were 12m long and had Plaxton's new Paramount body with shallower, square-cornered side windows and a short feature window before the waistline sloped down to the windscreen. A door is provided on the offside behind the rear wheels for use on continental tours. The Volvo/Plaxton combination was effectively the Wallace Arnold standard for the rest of the 1980s. *M Fowler*

This 1977 Leyland Leopard PSU4 was damaged in an accident in 1980 and withdrawn from service. In 1982 it emerged with a new 45-seat Plaxton body and was allocated to the Devon fleet. The body is only 7ft 6in wide and although using standard Supreme side windows was in fact built by Scarborough's service division, not by the main coachbuilding plant. Excursions advertised on the blackboards in the background include Exeter and Plymouth. The latter cost £3.25. *G H Truran*

Six Setra integral coaches were purchased in 1982-83. The German-built Setra was at that time the most expensive coach available in Britain and one of the pair delivered in 1983 was entered in the British Coach Rally. Driver and coach pause after the driving tests on Madeira Drive. The Setra had a rear-mounted Mercedes-Benz engine. *G R Mills*

Fourteen Bova Europa integrals were delivered in 1983, bringing the company's Bova fleet to 29 coaches - the largest in the country then or since. No more were bought by Wallace Arnold although consideration was given to trying the Futura, which succeeded the Europa, for the 1984 season. One Bova was painted in yellow Go Bananas livery for operation on the company's short-lived young persons' holiday tour programme of the same name. It is seen at Dover when new. *G R Mills*

In 1985 and 1986 the Devon fleet took delivery of Volvo B10Ms with Dutch-built Berkhof Esprite bodywork. There were 11 in all, the last of which was withdrawn in 1990. These coaches had cherished registration numbers, purchased to disguise their age. This one is seen on tour in Whitby in the summer of 1990. These were Wallace Arnold's first Volvos with bodywork by a builder other than Duple or Plaxton. *G R Mills*

After the take over in 1987 of Bee-Line's operations a few coaches received appropriate fleet names, including this 1985 Volvo B10M with Plaxton Paramount II bodywork. Note the use of a WA registration. *G H Truran*

An unusual addition to the Devon fleet in 1983 was this six-month-old Mercedes Benz L608D with 25-seat Plaxton body. The coach, built by Plaxton's service division, was a former Plaxton demonstrator. It is seen on an excursion in Brixham in 1989. *G R Mills*

Another coach with bodywork by a mainland European builder was this Volvo B10M, new in 1984 to Parks of Hamilton and purchased by Wallace Arnold in 1986. The body is by Van Hool of Belgium. When it joined the Wallace Arnold fleet it had been re-registered with a WA registration mark. *G R Mills*

The compact Viana coach used an Italian Iveco chassis and a Portuguese Caetano body. Two were added to the fleet in 1986 and one is seen here in Scarborough two years later. The logo alongside the fleetname was a short-lived combination of the WA initials and an outline of Scarborough castle. *M Fowler*

The mid-1980s saw a small number of leading British operators providing coaches on contract to Wallace Arnold which were painted in the company's livery. Southdown Motor Services, based in Sussex and one of the south coast's premier operators, ran this Leyland Tiger with Plaxton body on contract to the company. It is seen leaving Keswick on a Lake District and Trossachs holiday in 1987. Prior to the formation of the National Bus Company in 1969 Southdown, which became an NBC subsidiary, had been one of Wallace Arnold's major competitors offering high-quality coach holidays from London and the south east of England. *G B Wise*

Parks of Hamilton, Scotland's biggest coach operator, had hired coaches to Wallace Arnold from 1972 and in the 1980s painted a number in Wallace Arnold livery. These included rare Duple Calypso coaches, built on rear-engined Bova underframes with DAF engines. Four are seen lined up ready for delivery at Duple's Blackpool factory. *Duple*

Parks also provided under contract the biggest coach ever operated by Wallace Arnold, a three-axle DAF SBR3000 with double-deck Plaxton Paramount 4000 bodywork. It seated 74 passengers and still had space for a washroom. The chassis is rear-engined – a 284bhp DAF unit – and the space above the rear wheels formed a large luggage compartment. *D Akrigg*

Double-deck bus operation was reintroduced to the Wallace Arnold fleet in 1986 after a gap of almost 20 years. Two Park Royal-bodied Leyland Atlanteans, originally operated in Manchester, were purchased from Kirkby, the bus and coach dealer, and converted to open-top by Plaxton. They then joined the Hardwick's fleet and provided a seafront service in Scarborough. *K Lane*

Perhaps the most intriguing contracted coach was this Leyland Royal Tiger Doyen, supplied by East Yorkshire Motor Services. Wallace Arnold had considered buying Doyens but, perhaps anticipating the model's short production life, decided not to - this picture shows what a Wallace Arnold Doyen would have looked like. The Doyen was a high-specification rear-engined integral coach which was initially built by Charles H Roe in Leeds (a Leyland subsidiary) and then at Leyland's Workington plant. Sales volumes were low and the model was only produced for seven years. *G R Mills*

In 1987 Wallace Arnold bought two examples of Volvo's exclusive C10M. The C10M shared much of its mechanical componentry with the B10M chassis but incorporated in an integral structure manufactured in Switzerland by Ramseier & Jenzer. With a list price of £99,950 it was one of the most expensive coaches available in Britain at the time - so expensive that only ten were sold to UK operators. A standard Plaxton-bodied Volvo B10M cost around £80,000. *Stewart J Brown*

Four Mercedes Benz 307Ds joined the fleet in 1987 and two were allocated to Devon for use on tour feeders, bringing passengers in from outlying villages to join holiday tour coaches. Yeates of Loughborough equipped the 307Ds with high-backed coach seats for 12 passengers. *G R Mills*

Duple made an effort to regain some of Wallace Arnold's business in 1987 and supplied seven high-floor 340 bodies on Volvo B10M chassis. They were the company's last Duple bodies. *Stewart J Brown*

Another option considered by Wallace Arnold in 1987 was Hungarian-built Ikarus bodywork. Three Ikarus-bodied Volvos were operated for three seasons. The Ikarus body was known as the Blue Danube and was 3.6m high. One is seen on tour in Princes Street, Edinburgh. *G B Wise*

The last buses added to the Hardwick's fleet were two second-hand Leyland National integrals, bought from Greater Manchester Transport. One is seen in Scarborough bus station in the summer of 1988, by which time the Hardwick's operation had been sold to East Yorkshire Motor Services. *M Fowler*

In 1988 the order for new Plaxton-bodied Volvos was increased to cater for the newly-acquired Cotter operations and 12 coaches were delivered in a distinctive white and orange livery for use on Cotter's tours from Scotland. One pauses in Colchester on its way to Yugoslavia. *G R Mills*

1989 was another record year for Volvo, who delivered 49 B10Ms, all with Plaxton bodies, now of the improved Paramount III design. Most were high-floor 3500s, as seen here at Chester's Westminster Hotel. They brought to 205 the number of Volvo coaches delivered to Wallace Arnold since 1980. *K Lane*

Towards 2000

In 1926 my Grandfather, Robert Barr, started a family tradition, to provide quality holidays. Whilst holidays of today have changed dramatically, this tradition of customer care and value for money remains at the heart of our company's philosophy.
Robert A Barr, writing in the introduction to Wallace Arnold's 1996 holidays brochure

DESPITE THE ECONOMIC recession which gripped Britain at the start of the 1990s, Wallace Arnold maintained its extensive holiday tour programme, its investment in new coaches - and its profitability.

While some of its competitors were forced to cut back, Wallace Arnold continued to woo the markets which it had targetted as offering continued growth and in particular the over-55s. Britain has an ageing population and older people were generally less hard-hit by the economic downturn.

Indeed some areas provided growth opportunities. One was Southern Ireland with a combination of coach/sea and coach/air holidays. On the European mainland the majority of holidays were run by the company's own vehicles, although that did not prevent the promotion of new links taking advantage of France's prestigious high-speed train, the TGV, to whisk holidaymakers south from Paris after being taken there by coach from Britain. On most of these holidays Wallace Arnold's own coaches were waiting to collect travellers from the trains and to provide local excursions.

And with the opening of the Channel Tunnel in 1994, new holidays were promoted using the Eurostar train service to take travellers under the Channel rather than over it. Wallace Arnold coaches were used for the remainder of the holiday. When coach-carrying services were provided through the Tunnel from 1995, Wallace Arnold used these an alternative to the ferries on some holidays. For holidaymakers who enjoyed the opportunity to spend time at sea the company used a new cruise ferry service run by P&O from Portsmouth to Bilbao as an alternative to travelling by coach through France to get to Spain.

Some of the changes in Europe were less positive. Strife in what had been Yugoslavia brought a sad and sudden end to that country as a holiday destination. But in its place new areas have opened up and Wallace Arnold was quick to offer coach holidays to the newly-independent Baltic States and to Russia. With the rapid changes which have taken place in Eastern Europe these new holidays have proved popular - although they do revive memories of the pioneering spirit which prevailed in the early days of continental coach holidays. Border crossings are not always quite as slick as they are in Western Europe. And each coach goes abroad with a generous supply of water - not just for the use of the tour customers, but also to replenish the coach's cooling system if need be. Experience has shown that impurities in Eastern European water can be just as detrimental to the well-being of a coach as they can to its passengers...

Nearer home holidays to the Isle of Man were re-introduced in 1993, using locally-owned coaches for touring on the island. This represented but a small part of a steadily growing British Isles holiday programme.

At the start of the decade Wallace Arnold's standard coach was the proven Volvo/Plaxton combination. But the Plaxton Paramount body was nearing the end of its production life and totally new models were being developed to replace it.

These would bring yet higher standards of safety and comfort than the range they were replacing. The body frame was designed to meet strict new legislation on structural strength, while passenger comfort would be enhanced by features such as tinted double-glazing.

The new models were launched in 1991 as the Premiere and Excalibur, the latter designed as an expensive low-volume flagship coach. Wallace Arnold was among the first operators to order the new models taking 50 Premieres and 11 Excaliburs for the 1992 holiday season.

The first Excalibur was used to help launch the new range at Coach & Bus 91, the major transport trade show held at the National Exhibition Centre. And it was no ordinary coach. Wallace Arnold had it built to a very high specification with 26 cream leather-trimmed seats, tables, air-conditioning, on-board telephone (at a time when this was still an unusual feature) and a washroom. A centrally-positioned catering area which included a microwave oven separated the front and rear compartments of the coach, each of which had its own independent sound system complete with compact disc player. There was also a television and video installation with four screens. With a price tag approaching £150,000 it was the most expensive coach ever bought by Wallace Arnold. The standard specification coaches ordered at the same time cost around £100,000 each. Among the Excalibur's duties was the provision of transport for the Leeds United football team.

The remaining 60 new Plaxton-bodied Volvos

The last Plaxton Paramounts were delivered at the start of the 1990s. Among the 1990 intake were five which looked much like the remainder of the fleet but were in fact based on Mercedes-Benz rear-engined underframes. The German manufacturer's famous three-pointed star is carried on the front grille. *Plaxton*

were delivered in 1992, but while the new bodies offered a number of benefits in terms of safety and style, their introduction had put a lot of pressure on Plaxton's production facilities which resulted in late deliveries - the last six coaches arrived so late in the year that they had post-August 1 K-prefix registrations - and a few teething problems.

An unusual coach delivered in 1992 was the company's second Dennis Javelin. These were the first Dennises to run for Wallace Arnold for over 30 years. They had Plaxton Premiere bodies similar to those on the Volvos, but featured the standard Dennis drive-train with a vertical mid-mounted Cummins C-series engine driving through a ZF manual gearbox. The javelins were taken for evaluation alongside the company's standard Volvo products. Four minicoaches - two Mercedes-Benz and two Volkswagens - were bought primarily for feeder work. The Mercedes, based at Torquay, were also used on sightseeing tours which passed through picturesque Cockington, a village with restrictions on full-size coaches.

After the difficulties experienced in 1992, for 1993 Wallace Arnold cut its Plaxton body order from a planned 60 to just five, giving its long-standing supplier a chance to iron out the problems. Consequently the bulk of the company's business went to two new suppliers, Belgian coachbuilders Van Hool and Jonckheere. Van Hool got an order for 25 of its established Alizee body, while Jonckheere supplied 20 of its Deauville coach. All of the 1993 coaches were on Volvo B10M chassis.

In 1994 body orders were again split three ways, with Plaxton recovering some lost ground. The company added 63 Volvo B10Ms to its fleet with bodywork by Jonckheere on 27, Plaxton on 21 and Van Hool on 15. The Plaxton bodies were all high-specification Excaliburs. Two rather different Volvos were also purchased. One was a rear-engined B6 midicoach with a 35-seat Jonckheere body which was based in Leeds and used primarily to provide a feeder service from outlying towns to main departure points. The Scottish-built B6 had a 5.48-litre Volvo engine rated at 180bhp. The other non-standard Volvo was an altogether more impressive machine, a three-axle B12T with high-floor 50-seat Jonckheere body. It was intended to be one of five, but because of delivery delays the others were changed to standard B10Ms before being built.

The logic behind the three-axle layout of the B12T was that it allowed higher weights to be carried - and as coaches got increasingly sophisticated, so weight started to become an area to be watched. Wallace Arnold was also keen to gain operating experience of the heavier and more expensive B12T in anticipation of future changes in legislation which would allow the use of coaches over 12m long, a change which would require the use of three axles to cope with the higher weights involved. Although powered by a big 12-litre engine mounted in the rear overhang, the B12T's fuel consumption worked out at around the same as on the 9.6-litre B10Ms which formed the backbone of the fleet.

Another new type to be tried in 1994 was the Portuguese-built Caetano Optimo 21-seat midicoach, based on a Toyota chassis. Two were bought for tour feeder work.

An unusual purchase in 1994 saw the re-introduction of a double-deck bus to the fleet. However this was no ordinary double-decker, but a 30-year-old open-topper. It was a Leyland Titan PD3 with bodywork by Northern Counties, a survivor from a fleet supplied to Southdown Motor Services in Brighton. Repainted in Wallace Arnold colours and christened Uncle Wally, it was bought to take tour passengers from their hotel in Babbacombe into Torquay. In between hotel transfers it was used successfully to run sightseeing tours around Torquay in the long-standing tradition of English coastal resorts. Despite its age, the elderly Titan performed faultlessly. It also proved totally reliable when called upon to perform duties in Leeds, such as taking part in local parades, trundling the 300-plus miles up the motorway (and another 300-plus back again) with no trouble at all. Such was the success of Uncle Wally that a second, similar, open-topper was acquired in 1996.

In 1995 the new coach intake saw a return to standardisation with just one order, which called for 35 Volvo B10Ms, all with Plaxton bodywork. Six were Excaliburs; the balance Premieres. And for 1996 Wallace Arnold once again standardised on the proven Volvo/Plaxton combination, taking delivery of no fewer than 51 new coaches - an investment of around £7 million to maintain the high standards of comfort and safety which the

Plaxton's new generation coach body is the present-day Wallace Arnold standard, and by 1996 the company had purchased almost 200 of the type. Most have been Premieres on Volvo B10M chassis, but this Premier is unusual in the Wallace Arnold fleet in being mounted on a Dennis Javelin. *Dennis*

A number of the new Plaxton coaches delivered in the 1990s have been Excaliburs, which are easily identifiable by the use of a deep, swept-back, windscreen. Two 1995 Volvo B10Ms with Excalibur bodies are posed at Scarborough before being delivered. *Plaxton*

Left: Volvo's midi-sized B6 coach is relatively rare. This one, with Jonckheere body, was operated for a short period in 1994. It was a 35-seater.

Below, left: At the other extreme Wallace Arnold tried the Volvo B12T, the company's first three-axle coach since the Bedford VAL of the 1960s. This, too, was bodied by Jonckheere.

Yet despite this, at the start of 1996 the government introduced legislation which prohibited coaches from using the outside lane of Britain's motorways. Seen by some as a ploy to make coach travel less attractive at a time when British Rail was being privatised, it presents another new challenge for coach operators who forecast that the restriction will make it harder to predict journey times - and may see coaches on some routes reverting to A-roads which, of course, is where long-distance coach touring started.

But it is successfully meeting challenges like this which have made Wallace Arnold a household name for quality and value-for-money coaching throughout Great Britain - and beyond. And whatever the future holds there can be little doubt that the company will continue developing new ways of helping its customers enjoy their leisure in the highest standards of safety and comfort.

The modern coaches which Wallace Arnold is running in the 1990s have little in common with the first charabancs which Robert Barr ran 70 years before. But the company's aims remain the same: the provision of a high-quality service to each and every one of its customers. There's still a Robert Barr at the company's helm - Robert A Barr, grandson of the founder, and now Chairman of Wallace Arnold Tours, following in the footsteps of his grandfather and uncle before him. Few companies which are household names throughout Britain - and beyond - can demonstrate

company's customers expect.

To mark 70 years of operation, 1996 saw a number of the company's holidays featuring gala birthday dinners. A 70th anniversary celebration tour was also added to the company's extensive list of holidays - 15 days round Britain from £599.

Coaches are proven to be the safest means of road transport. Their drivers have to pass a tough driving test to get a Passenger Carrying Vehicle (PCV) licence, and companies like Wallace Arnold invest time and money in training which embraces everything from road safety to customer care.

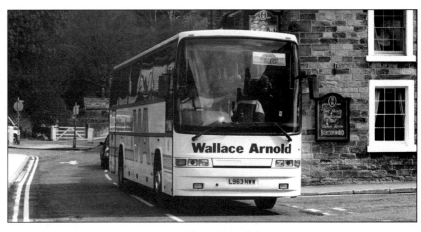

Forty Volvo B10Ms with Van Hool Alizee bodies were added to the fleet in 1993-94.

Standard Johnckheere bodies were supplied on 47 Volvo B10Ms in the early 1990s. One is seen on tour in the Peak District. *Stewart J Brown*

The opening of the Channel Tunnel brought new opportunities including, from 1995, the option to take coaches through the tunnel on specially-built trains as an alternative to using the cross-Channel ferries. A Jonckheere-bodied Volvo edges its way onto the train in Kent.

Although based in Devon, this veteran open-top Leyland Titan is used for special events around the country. It is seen here in Leeds in 1995.

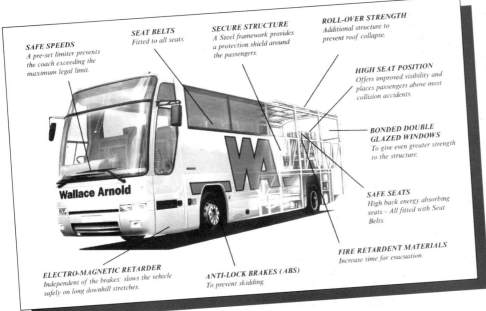

SAFE SPEEDS
A pre-set limiter prevents the coach exceeding the maximum legal limit.

SEAT BELTS
Fitted to all seats.

SECURE STRUCTURE
A Steel framework provides a protection shield around the passengers.

ROLL-OVER STRENGTH
Additional structure to prevent roof collapse.

HIGH SEAT POSITION
Offers improved visibility and places passengers above most collision accidents.

BONDED DOUBLE GLAZED WINDOWS
To give even greater strength to the structure.

SAFE SEATS
High back energy absorbing seats - All fitted with Seat Belts.

FIRE RETARDENT MATERIALS
Increase time for evacuation.

ELECTRO-MAGNETIC RETARDER
Independent of the brakes: slows the vehicle safely on long downhill stretches.

ANTI-LOCK BRAKES (ABS)
To prevent skidding.

Wallace Arnold is proud of its record for operating safe, reliable and comfortable coaches. A cutaway drawing of an Excalibur in the company's 1996 holiday brochures is used to highlight some of the inbuilt safety features of both the Plaxton body and the Volvo chassis.

Summary of new deliveries from 1926

YEAR	AEC	LEYLAND	VOLVO	BEDFORD	FORD	OTHERS	TOTAL	YEAR	AEC	LEYLAND	VOLVO	BEDFORD	FORD	OTHERS	TOTAL
1926	-	1	-	-	-	-	1	1970	-	25	-	1	2	-	28
1927	-	5	-	-	-	-	5	1971	8	29	-	2	3	1[10]	43
1928	-	1	-	-	-	5[1]	6	1972	1	32	-	5	-	-	38
1929	-	1	-	-	-	-	1	1973	-	27	-	14	-	-	41
								1974	-	40	-	10	-	-	50
1930	-	3	-	-	-	1[2]	4	1975	-	27	-	11	-	6[11]	44
1931	-	3	-	-	-	-	3	1976	-	25	-	1	-	-	26
1932	-	2	-	-	-	-	2	1977	-	29	-	2	6	-	37
1933	1	3	-	-	-	-	4	1978	-	35	6	2	-	-	43
1934	2	1	-	-	-	-	3	1979	-	20	16	-	-	-	36
1935	-	4	-	-	-	-	4								
1936	-	3	-	-	-	4[3]	7	1980	-	20	18	1	15	-	54
1937	-	4	-	-	-	1[4]	5	1981	-	38	-	1	15	-	54
1938	-	4	-	1	-	-	5	1982	-	-	6	-	-	19[12]	25
1939	-	4	-	-	-	-	4	1983	-	-	17	2	-	16[13]	35
								1984	-	-	6	-	-	-	6
1940	-	3	-	-	-	-	3	1985	-	-	11	-	-	-	11
1941	-	-	-	-	-	-	-	1986	-	-	32	-	-	3[14]	35
1942	-	-	-	-	-	-	-	1987	-	-	26	-	-	-	26
1943	-	-	-	6	-	-	6	1988	-	-	40	-	-	-	40
1944	-	-	-	6	-	-	6	1989	-	-	49	-	-	-	49
1945	-	-	-	-	-	-	-								
1946	1	2	-	1	-	-	4	1990	-	-	52	-	-	7[15]	59
1947	8	22	-	17	-	2[5]	49	1991	-	-	57	-	-	1[4]	58
1948	2	8	-	8	-	2[5]	20	1992	-	-	61	-	-	1[4]	62
1949	8	8	-	6	-	7[6]	29	1993	-	-	50	-	-	-	50
								1994	-	-	65	-	-	2[16]	67
1950	5	8	-	2	-	-	15	1995	-	-	35	-	-	-	35
1951	3	10	-	4	-	-	17	1996	-	-	51	-	-	2[16]	53
1952	5	8	-	1	-	4[7]	18								
1953	1	8	-	6	-	-	15								
1954	20	3	-	3	-	1[8]	27								
1955	13	-	-	-	-	6[9]	19								
1956	6	10	-	-	-	7[8]	23								
1957	6	1	-	-	-	1[8]	8								
1958	23	6	-	-	-	-	29								
1959	24	-	-	1	1	-	26								
1960	24	2	-	6	15	-	47								
1961	19	8	-	-	18	-	45								
1962	9	14	-	-	6	-	29								
1963	7	16	-	6	8	-	37								
1964	3	18	-	18	3	2[2]	44								
1965	5	20	-	18	7	-	50								
1966	21	2	-	18	9	-	50								
1967	3	15	-	10	1	-	29								
1968	4	17	-	10	-	-	31								
1969	-	35	-	10	-	-	45								

The above figures do not include minibuses or minicoaches of under 20 seats, of which 54 were purchased new between 1960 and 1987, typically at the rate of three a year. Most (42 out of the 54) were Bedfords.

Notes on other chassis makes:
1 Two Albions, two Tilling-Stevens and one Dennis.
2 Albion.
3 Two Dennis and two Maudslays.
4 Dennis.
5 Daimler.
6 Six Daimlers and one Guy.
7 Three Commers and one Maudslay.
8 Commer.
9 Five Commers and one Sentinel.
10 Mercedes-Benz.
11 Bristol.
12 Fifteen Bovas and four Setras.
13 Fourteen Bovas and two Setras.
14 One DAF and two Ivecos.
15 Five Mercedes-Benz and two DAFs.
16 Toyota.